School Law

THE LIBRARY OF EDUCATION

A Project of The Center for Applied Research in Education, Inc.

G. R. Gottschalk, Director

Categories of Coverage

I	II	III
Curriculum and Teaching	Administration, Organization, and Finance	Psychology for Educators

IV	V	VI
History, Philosophy, and Social Foundations	Professional Skills	Educational Institutions

School Law

WARREN E. GAUERKE

Professor of
Educational Administration
Wayne State University

The Center for Applied Research in Education, Inc.
New York

Foreword

The growing importance of school law is reflected by the growing interest in school law. Several decades ago teachers, school administrators, school board members, and even school business officials were not too much concerned about the legal side of public school administration. Questions regarding the legality of school affairs were the sole concern of lawyers and solicitors.

Today the situation is quite different. Deep and broad interest in school law abounds. School officials, school employees, and others connected with the public schools want at least to understand the basic elements of school law. There is considerable evidence of a growing interest in school law, particularly that which is based upon judicial decisions. It is apparent at the national, state, and local levels.

Lawyers need not be alarmed that the "do it yourself" trend in the school law field will deprive them of business. On the contrary, the more one knows about school law, the more likely he is to know when legal counsel by professional lawyers is needed.

Several decades ago only a few of the largest universities scheduled discrete courses in school law, but now a hundred or more institutions of higher learning claim to offer courses that deal with the legal aspects of education.

The numerous state and national conferences dealing with school law, and the National Organization on Legal Problems of Education, established in 1954, give further evidence of the increased concern about school law.

The most convincing evidence of the growing interest in school law, however, is the growing body of literature dealing with the subject. Dozens of articles treating various phases of school law are published each year in professional journals. Each year additional books on school law are published.

Obviously, there is duplication of topics and legal principles referred to in other publications. This book contains many chapters and sections appearing elsewhere. Significantly, the first three chapters deal with matters not now included in other school law publications. The first two chapters on sources and on scope are not presently found in most texts.

With some modifications, the outline for this volume is used by the author for teaching school law. The coverage should make it acceptable for others who teach school law; it is a book that everyone interested in school law would want to have in his library.

EDWARD C. BOLMEIER
Professor of Education
Duke University

School Law

Warren E. Gauerke

A web of law underlies all educational systems, and this is particularly true of the public schools. *School Law*, by Warren E. Gauerke, is a careful study of the legal structure which undergirds public education.

While this book covers the conventional topics of the law related to public schools, it has, in addition, an excellent introductory section on the legal heritage from both the ancient world and Western Europe. This material is not to be found in any other text on school law.

As one reads this book, he is struck by the degree to which the law has penetrated all aspects of education. The organization of education has firm bases in the law, as do relations with pupils, teachers, and other employees. The general problem of liability is covered thoroughly; chapters are devoted to negligence, individual members of the board of education, and school employees. This book might well be read in conjunction with the other Library of Education volumes on administration.

This book is designed to develop an understanding of the law and education, and it is more than a set of annotations from legal briefs and cases. While these are referred to, the book could stand on its basic discussion of the principles of school law.

The book also stresses the fact that educators should have an understanding of the law but should not be amateur lawyers. Careful advice is given as to the seeking of expert legal aid. This book helps to establish a sound rationale in law for the educator.

Dr. Warren E. Gauerke is professor of educational administration at Wayne State University. He has been very active nationally in professional organizations, especially in the National Organization on Legal Problems in Education. Dr. Gauerke is well qualified to write this volume on school law.

DANIEL E. GRIFFITHS
Content Editor

Contents

CHAPTER I

Sources of the Law

Introduction

The profession of teaching, including the administration of schools, has its basis in law. It rests upon ideas of the "democratic state" and relationships existing between the school and state.

Many agree that knowledge of school law is essential for personnel of public schools and for others as well. It provides answers to questions which plague individuals and institutions. Such questions involve differences on civil rights, segregation of races, loyalty and subversion, and separation of church and state.

Law literally means an edict or order, and it refers to more than regulations and statutes which provide the framework. The real law, or justice, is made up of a code and equity. Law is the rigid written framework which states "what is legal." Equity, or fair play, sees that law does not produce an unfair result.

Reasons for the study of school law are many. With school litigation increasing, additional opportunities for examining school law problems need to be provided. A reading of cases (and discussion of them) mentioned in this monograph will aid the reader in grasping legal principles.

Judicial pronouncements cited here illustrate the reasoning of higher courts with respect to public education. One should not seek answers to legal questions; rather, he should seek principles as applied to a set of facts. How such principles came into being is a fascinating chronicle, told in a volume by a member of the New York Bar.[1] Besides writing about legal problems, past and present, Wormser provides details of the lives of persons which have helped to give law shape and substance.

---

[1] Rene A. Wormser, *The Law* (New York: Simon and Schuster, Inc., 1949), pp. 1–610. Here is the story of lawmakers and "the law" we have lived by, from earliest times to the present. This Columbia Law School graduate surveys, as few others have managed, the development of our legal institutions. He makes legal matters understandable to nonlawyers. The reader soon loses himself in the chronicle of the law which had beginnings in ancient civilizations and which has grown steadily in its breadth and depth.

Legal Heritage from the Ancient World

To primitive man, "wrath of the gods" was real. It was not wise to antagonize the headman or the group.[2]

For ages, man was controlled only by accumulated experience which he followed unconsciously. There was no law for a long time. When hurt, the primitive wanted only revenge against his attacker and against the "thing" which hurt him.

Man developed legal machinery only recently. Early peoples used clan assemblies as courts and legislatures. The idea that the clan chief should attempt to prevent wrongdoing was a last step in the development of primitive law.

With awarding of damages for injury, some sort of court became necessary. The first was merely a peacemaker and might be ignored. However, it became less likely that the judgment of a chief would be ignored since he presided over the court. Legal custom came to be a part of the taboo system, this "law" compelling early man to conduct himself properly.

When tribal law was put into written form, the lay jurist was needed. In turn, a "philosophy of the law" was developed which freed the law from religious biases.

The law of the Greeks. Ancient Greek law was derived from primitive customs and was molded by Mesopotamian, Egyptian, and other influences. Socrates helped produce today's "case method." For example, a professor engages the legal student in argumentation by stating facts; he requests answers, and from the answers ensues the Socratic conversation. The Greeks also had a land recording system which is intelligible to any modern title-searcher.[3]

They did not have as systematic an approach to law as did the Romans; their plan used the jury as judge also. The head of the Greek clan used adult males of the clan as a "lower assembly," this consultative assembly being the ancestor of today's lower legislative house.

After Homer (900 B.C.), men of laws collected customs and put them into written form; such "usages" then became man-made laws. To quiet unrest, Draco was commissioned to make new laws and have all laws written down for the first time.

---

[2] *Ibid.*, p. 4. This idea and many others included in Chapter I come directly from Wormser's work, *The Law.*

[3] Wormser, *op. cit.*, p. 60.

The law of the Jews. The contribution of the Jews was the Torah and Pentateuch, both adopted by Christianity as part of its law. The Ten Commandments, the "Moses as Lawgiver" idea, the concept of vengeance, and knowledge of land and family are Jewish legacies.

The *Code of Hammurabi* is the only complete pre-Hebrew code of law from which the Jews borrowed much. The Talmud, a compilation of laws for Jews, is unlike modern legal codes in that it is not a code in any logical manner; it is "interspersed with poetical, religious, and philosophical disgressions. . . ."[4]

Jewish law made no distinction between religious and civil rules. It held that an understanding of all law—religious, social, and legal —was necessary to a proper comprehension of rules to govern human conduct.[5]

The Torah is concerned with civil or private wrongs and is the "constitution" of Jewish law. The Talmud contains a collection of the law and bears a similar relation to the Torah as common law does to English law. In old Jewish law one was not held responsible if he knew not that his ox was dangerous when it gored a man. Only when one kept an animal which he knew was likely to harm another was he held accountable. It took a long time for humans to understand the concept of negligence.[6]

Changes in mores made it possible for legal customs to be accommodated without any actual law-making bodies. When the "eye for an eye" law had gone too far, beginnings of a judicial system appeared. A basic precept of the Jewish legal system was that "the law" must remain unchanged, but Jewish jurists managed to rationalize in order to justify new rules. Wormser[7] states that "no other people have been so adept at taking a . . . phrase . . . and rationalizing upon it a . . . structure of law as did the ancient Jews."

The law of the Jews became a chief source of the law of Continental Europe and England. The law of Moses influenced the creation of an American legal system. Some colonial communities were ruled under Old Testament law.

---

[4] *Ibid.*, p. 23.

[5] *Ibid.*, p. 25.

[6] *Ibid.*, p. 20. In Exodus XXI, pp. 28 and 29, the notion of negligence appears. Curiously enough, according to the Bible, an ox had to be stoned to death and its flesh uneaten if it gored a man. In England the tree from which a man fell was considered to be "an accursed thing." If a man drowned in a well, that well had to be filled.

[7] *Ibid.*, p. 5.

The law of the Romans.   This law is one of the most important of many influences producing Western law. Students of Latin know of the marvels of Roman government, the twelve tables, and contributions of Cicero and Crassus.

It was about the year 200 B.C. that Catus published "the first lawbook" in Western Europe. It reflected Roman sophistication in legal matters. After this volume, writing on legal matters became more frequent, and public interest mounted. The upper classes in Rome produced what some consider to have been "the most remarkable governmental and legal system of all time." Before their collapse, the Romans had developed their jurisprudence to a high degree of specialization.

What today is classified as "negligence," the Romans divided into several categories.[8] They perceived the notion of contributory fault and had the idea of culpability. This they divided into gross negligence and minor carelessness.

The Roman city magistrate of Empire days had charge of the administration of justice. He employed general principles of law which were universal. Legal leeway came also when the Romans borrowed the Greek concept of "natural law." Jurists expressed their opinions openly and thus assisted in widened application of laws. Roman lawyers could practice only by being licensed. However, a good legal system did not make the Romans a moral people, for they found ways to violate the harsh Julian Laws.[9]

Roman law astounds the modern reader with its magnificent structure built without benefit of legislation by an assembly. In fact, the legal student of today constantly wonders at the modern direction of Roman law. Different from Americans who borrowed the wisdom of others, the Romans used few alien materials to erect their astounding legal structure. With very few alterations, their invented law could be our law today.

Roman and canon law.   Not until the collapse of the Western half of the Roman Empire in the latter half of the fifth century could the Papacy think seriously about being independent from secular support. When the vast Empire did fall, the popes became temporal rulers of a part of the once sprawling realm. Then it was that the canon or Church law truly became a civil law. From this

---

[8] *Ibid.,* pp. 135–137. Our word "injury" comes from the Roman *iniuria,* which means an injury to a person himself, differing from a *furtum,* a trespass against his property.

[9] *Ibid.,* p. 118.

era forward, canon law greatly influenced the lives of Europeans.

When the Roman law did not conflict with the Scriptures and Judeo-Christian moral principles, early Church fathers would use it. The Church-adopted Roman law was not the classic or "pure" law, however, and a conflict developed between the canon and Roman systems. Wormser states that the Roman law won out, but only after canon law had made deep inroads into European legal systems.

Legal Heritage from Western Europe

Germanic and barbarian law.   In the immediate post-Empire centuries, the Germans had held their land entirely by means of clans. This system provided much chance for strife and feuding. The Germanic peoples had much interest in their trials, which were public.

In the early "Dark Ages" in England, law was based on organizations called the "hundreds." These groups were divided into groups of ten families, each responsible for maintaining order. Decisions were rendered by delegates from the "hundreds." The presiding officer instructed the others as to what law they were to apply. Generally, he was an ecclesiastic and was influenced by the Church on legal interpretations. On the Continent, the Germanic codes were adulterated and written in Latin. Codifiers who were willing to introduce innovations into the Germanic law were clerics influenced by Roman legal heritage. Almost perversely, English laws were written in German. They remained German with little change until the Norman conquest. It is for this reason that some have called the English "the most German people on earth."

The concept of "folkright" persisted after the breakup of Germanic clans, due to invasions. The idea of actual individual rights instead of group rights was born and flourished early in England. In fact, the only group to which William the Conqueror attached himself in his arbitrary rule was a hand-picked council of advisers. William would tolerate no other group—no parliament.

During the Middle Ages, laws of one village varied considerably from those of its neighbor. Therefore, several local legal systems operated at one time. Germanic law was meager and not uniform. Roman law, however, was carefully developed and became the stronger after the two systems merged.

English law.   Although English law developed almost independently of Continental Europe, it was mixed with some Continental law. It grew into a system that was the antecedent of American law.

During the reign of Henry VIII (1491–1547), a proposal was made to have the Roman law adopted in England. At this time also, Scotland adopted large sections of this law. King Henry wanted nothing to do with "foreign" influences, especially those with the adjective "Roman" attached to them.

American law was shaped by Continental, Jewish, and English law, and the period which produced Elizabeth I was important to its development. The legitimacy of Henry's offspring was questioned. The Puritan movement was fostered by sharp religious turmoil, starting during Henry VIII's dominion. Harsh laws came to New England.

Despite conflict with secular law, Church law had some wholesome results. Canon law helped shape the civil law in use today. Church courts developed many procedures which remain parts of modern law. It was the Church which put pleadings in writing, although the German ones were oral. Proof was sought out by witnesses and written evidence.

English kings helped to build the groundwork for absolutist rule. They used the "king's peace" to obtain order. The king could fine those who broke it. Whenever possible, an action was held to involve a breach of this peace; thus, the action would properly come within the jurisdiction of the king's courts rather than local ones.

During the thirteenth century, the unwritten British Constitution was being forged quite unconsciously. The Magna Carta contained principles developed as part of the English law over many subsequent centuries, and it served as one of the foundations of personal liberty of the English people. By the time of Henry VIII, British kings were proud to be "rulers by grace of God," but they were equally conscious that they ruled with the consent of Parliament.

The history of Western Europe is brighter because of legal development in England. During the Tudor reigns (from 1485 to 1603), British subjects had acquired rights based on ideas within the "great charter." These were not always defined precisely and did not provide the protection that Western man demands in the twentieth century. Likewise, the struggle of the common people for actual control of government had not been fully won by the 1700's.

The transition from Roman and Norman-French influences to

English customs (by the close of the Wars of the Roses, 1455–1485) aided the jury system in at least one way: About the fifteenth century, witnesses could testify in a tongue comprehensible to the jury, and lawyers could thus address juries.

Even though English law influenced that in the United States, one difference is apparent. In the United States a lawyer prepares the brief, takes it to the court, and may argue the merits before a jury. In England, the defender may be a solicitor who advises clients and prepares cases. He may appear as an advocate in the lower courts only, sometimes giving legal opinions on certain questions, but at his own risk. The solicitor may be sued for negligence. One cannot sue a barrister, no matter what errors he may make. He argues cases in all courts. In the United States, an attorney combines the two functions.

Specific Anglo-Saxon contributions.   Law of the Anglo-Saxons was like that of the ancient Code of Hammurabi, making distinctions between classes and paying higher compensations to an injured lord than to an injured freeman.

Valuable legacies from the Anglo-Saxons such as the writ of habeas corpus and freedom of speech, first appeared in the 1689 Act of Parliament. Another contribution was their jury system. They provided the *grand jury* to indict for crimes and the *petit jury* to sit at the trial of a case and to determine the facts. Now, when a jury is sitting, one of the features of English law is that the jury is the sole judge of the facts. The judge himself is the sole interpreter of what constitutes the law.

An additional inheritance from Anglo-Saxon law is the reasonable-man idea, which appears throughout criminal and civil law. When a person does an act, the true test to determine legal responsibility continues to be: "What would a reasonably prudent man, in the circumstances, anticipate to be the consequences of his act?"

Anglo-Saxon law included the rule of *stare decisis*—"to stand by decided cases." Under this theory, once a point of law has been decided by the highest court of appeal, it is fixed law and can be changed only by legislation.

Another legacy from Anglo-Saxon law is the "due process" concept, requiring that the court which assumes to determine the rights of parties shall have jurisdiction (the legal authority to require action) and that there shall be notice of the charges and opportunity for the defendant to be heard in his behalf.

Napoleonic law. As the direct result of Napoleon's support of legal reform in France, all of Western Continental Europe eventually adopted a codified legal system. Napoleon Bonaparte encouraged the commission he established to codify the French laws. The entire French bar contributed to the drafting of the *Civil Code*. It is this civil law which is called "Napoleonic" law. The codes worked over by the French Commission were later translated into almost every Western language and into many Eastern languages.

In the countries of Continental Europe, a judge has the codified law before him. He is bound only by its words. These he may interpret as he sees fit. Thus, under the Napoleonic or codified system of law, the judge may interpret the language of the written law almost as he wishes, regardless of precedent. A judge may feel obliged to base his immediate decision on the opinion of a famous jurist or a precedent set in another case. The Continental judge, reminds Wormser,[10] is never bound by previous decisions (no *stare decisis* rule).

The Common Law jurists wonder how growth of the law can occur when judicial decisions are not considered to be part of the law. In other words, a disadvantage is that the law ceases to grow under the code system. There are no findings of the courts to adjust the law and help make it work in accordance with changing views. One advantage of the Continental system, however, is that it enables a lawyer to practice law without needing access to tens of thousands of law books.

---

[10] *Ibid.*, p. 229.

CHAPTER II

Scope of School Law

Categories

Unwritten and written law. The words "unwritten" and "written" law refer to origin. All legislative enactments are part of written or planned law. This category includes constitutions, treaties, statutes, administrative rules, and municipal ordinances. What remains of the body of law after taking out these written parts is the "unwritten" law or judicial decisions. This law is unplanned, not deliberately created by authorized bodies as is the written law. For reference, it appears as printed material.

Experience provides evidence that it is not possible to establish written law (rules) for every conceivable situation. Decisions of courts cover such gaps. Legislative bodies have been content to leave such decisions untouched. This law reposes, not in statutes, but in tradition that has come down through the centuries.[1] None of this tradition is included in any law formulated by "lawmaking" bodies.

Written law has been designed as such by lawmakers. It embraces regulations of administrative bodies, ordinances, statutes, and constitutions. It has a certain rigidity about it. Despite this, man has managed to escape its inflexibilities and has suited written law to many changing conditions.

When people began writing their laws, abrupt changes took place. Written law had the chance to be understood and then become common knowledge. No longer could it be the monopoly of privileged classes as it had been with priests of the tribes. When the law was written for all to see, however, there was an end to its spontaneous development.

The common law. Other than the enormous mass of law in the United States which has been written down is unwritten law of

---

[1] Lewis Mayers, *The American Legal System* (New York: Harper & Row, Publishers, 1955), p. 350. In his footnote Professor Mayers adds that the term "unwritten" is not an apt one. The nonstatutory law is often referred to as "case law." There does not seem much likelihood that certain areas of the law—contracts, torts, agency, and some others—will shortly be removed from the category of traditional law and be reframed in the form of statute or written law.

another kind. It is the "common law," found in reports of decided cases. Some of it is unchanged from the form in which the law was originally created by early English judges.

The term "common law" implies law that is basic to all, consisting of a body of rules which has resulted from established customs being court enforced. Centuries ago, courts decided each case arbitrarily on what judges believed to be its merits. As similar cases arose, courts began to follow earlier cases as precedents. Thus developed the common law, administered by the courts and common to all English subjects, regardless of geography or social class. Today the great body of law is common law, and precedents are as vital a part of the fundamental law as legislative enactments.

Reasons for growth. English traveling judges believed that there was a rule of law which would cover the facts of a case. They believed that, with patience, such a rule could be discovered. A truly able judge could detect such a law and provide the solution.

By painless change, primitive and rudimentary rules were converted into modern legal tools. Borderline cases provided such opportunity, for judges had to struggle to delineate the borders and create a legal system which made sense within itself.[2] The opinion of a legal expert—in a case where a change had been effected— would be read and accepted by other jurists. These decisions then served as premises for further rationalization.

Early judges who relied upon their own reasoning were never totally free in creating law. They were bound by precedent, by pressures of a society into which decisions had to be fitted, and by their own limitations. They had inherited inconsistencies within the law. Justice Holmes stated that the law is always approaching, but never reaching, consistency. In his book, *The Common Law,* he remarked:

> Every important principle which is developed by litigation is in fact . . . the result of more or less definitely understood views of public policy; more generally . . . the unconscious result of instinctive preferences and inarticulate convictions, but none the less traceable to views of public policy. . . .

Confusion over terminology. There is no adequate basis for understanding fully such words as "customs" and "laws." Nobody knows precisely just what such words mean. Many definitions have been formulated. Not one is completely adequate for all situations.

Natural law was held to be a part of the existing order of things—

---

[2] Rene A. Wormser, *The Law,* p. 263.

that is, made up of principles that were fixed and permanent. Later on, written constitutions were demanded because people deemed them to possess superior dignity and force. They were supposed to mirror the principles of natural law. When marriage was no longer temporary but came to be a socially recognized and controlled institution, new terms were invented. As man progressed, life demanded other legal regulations. Thus grew the maritime law, international law, parliamentary law, and world law.

The modern law student studies such categories as administrative law, agency law, bills and notes, real and personal property, constitutional law, contracts, damages, evidence, future interests, labor law, sales, taxation, and torts. In his study he will come upon ceremonial law, moral law, Mosaic law, and organic law. There is also statute law which may abrogate a common law rule.

There is procedural law, covering rules under which one establishes his legal rights. What is left out of procedural law is the "substantive law." This category embraces such questions as what rights one has against a trespasser, who gets the property when a man dies, and what the penalty is for theft.

The phrase "the law" is a paradox. It is mountain-like in concept, but the smallest detail is highly relevant in specific instances. One should know the law as it affects him; yet, he can know so little.

Meaning and Origins of School Law

Scarcely a session of a state legislature can go by without the enactment of additional "school laws" which affect school personnel, real property, and financial support. "School law" means that body of legal precedent affecting education which comes from all sources. It includes more than state statutes which appear in the "School Code." If one were to stop here, he would overlook the relevant provisions of state and federal constitutions. He would not take cognizance of rules and regulations touching education authorized by administrative agencies. He would have omitted the thousands of policies adopted by local school boards which, when valid, amplify state and federal law.

School law is not legal precedent found in a book; neither is it a specific branch of the law like "Bills and Notes." Rather, it is the whole body of rules—from whatever source of the law—that pertains to education. Consequently, there are many school laws in each state. They provide one foundation for public education.

Up to 1940, many courses labeled "school law" were limited to looking at State Department publications and at the code for the legal requirements for certifying personnel. Since then, however, courses have provided opportunity to explore judicial interpretations and to delve into principles underlying statutes and decisions. Instructors increasingly have emphasized that the school is a social institution, subject to changing functions. Powers formerly believed unnecessary do become absolutely necessary.[3] The student is asked to view variation in statutes pertaining to schools, not content *per se*. He sees that lawmakers under pressure must improvise and thus construct new laws hastily.

Creators of school law work at state and local levels. Since legislatures delegate certain authority (within the scope of power set by the constitution and state statutes), school laws result from such delegation. They often prescribe details within fundamental principles. They may confer upon agents the authority to implement intent of principles. School laws are rules to be used as tools to aid school boards in the administration of schools.[4] They are not intended to be profound edicts and observed literally at all costs.

It was through school laws that Americans won the battle for tax support of public schools. These provided the means to eliminate the pauper-school, and they helped make schools free of tuition charges. Laws were enacted to establish state supervision of schools, to eliminate sectarianism in public schools, and to extend the system of public education beyond the high school.[5]

Types of school law. The thousands of school laws fall into four groups. (1) federal and state constitutional provisions; (2) federal and state statutory law (of which school codes are a part); (3) administrative rules and regulations (including federal, state, and local agencies of government); and (4) judge-made law.

Constitutional law. With few exceptions, state constitutions make it obligatory for legislatures to provide for "the establishment and maintenance of efficient systems" of public schools. However, certain constitutional rights based upon the federal Constitution

[3] Newton Edwards, *The Courts and the Public Schools* (Chicago: The University of Chicago Press, 1935), p. 147.

[4] Robert Hamilton, *The Bi-Weekly School Law Letter*, Vol. III, No. 17 (October 15, 1953), p. 66.

[5] Ellwood P. Cubberley, *Public Education in the United States* (Boston: Houghton Mifflin Company, 1919), pp. 128–129.

are guaranteed to citizens. They may not, for example, be deprived of privileges contained in the Fourteenth Amendment.[6] This amendment affords the citizen protection from infringements by the federal and state governments.

Statutory law. Any listing of federal and state laws affecting education would show how far-reaching this category is. On the federal level are laws such as "school lunch," "vocational rehabilitation," and the "G.I. Bill." All 50 states have plenary power over education, a fact evidenced by the thousands of school laws passed each year. The statute books contain legislation prescribing minimums regarding attendance, curriculums, and teaching credentials. Local school districts may exceed these if they so choose. State statutes are therefore the most-used single source of school law.

Administrative law. Regulations of agencies at all three levels of government—designed to implement constitutional and statutory law—are actually part of statutory law. As such, administrative codes and directives of governmental agents greatly influence the conduct of education.

In actual practice, legislatures delegate specific authority to other state and local agencies. For education, these can be the state department of education, tax commission, and tenure commission. There may be dozens of other state administrative bodies which affect educational policy.

At the federal level, despite state autonomy, there is administrative law which influences education. Such agencies are the National Labor Relations Board, Interstate Commerce Commission, Federal Communications Commission, and the Department of Agriculture. The Office of Education (within the Department of Health, Education, and Welfare) exercises authority over such functions as determining criteria for extending loans and research grants.

Judge-made law. Courts do much more than merely apply the law which legislatures create. They make new laws as effectively as legislatures. It would be impossible for a state legislature to provide laws for every conceivable situation. The ever-changing structure of life creates the need for new rules. The elaboration

---

[6] Even though a pupil is protected by provisions of the Amendment, each state is sovereign in the exercise of its police powers. The state has control of education. In the "Segregation" and subsequent cases it has appeared as though federal constitutional law—the "equal protection" clause—was being employed to alter education policy. The arena for upholding federal constitutional law happened to be the public schools, where citizens who were pupils also had rights protected.

of new rules "is an inescapable concomitant of the judicial process."[7]

The legal bases of public education. The meaning and origins of school law can be rendered intelligible by talking about "types" of school law. The legal bases are not types but correspond closely to the four divisions of school law described previously.

The "law" which has been accumulating since civilization began is of several kinds. The first category is federal and state constitutional law. The second is statutory law, including acts of administrative bodies. The third legal basis is the judge-made law (the decisions of federal and state appellate courts).

Constitutional law. The very foundation of the legal structure of public education is the constitution of each state which vests control in its legislature. State constitutions contain mention of public education in terms of specific and general statements.

The federal system rests squarely upon the division of powers between a nation and the several states. The national government is one of enumerated powers, delegated to it by the states. These delegated powers may be either express or implied. Action for all departments of the federal government must be based upon, and find support in, the Constitution. The distinctive feature of constitutional government is that powers of government are limited. Whether it be a delegated power of the nation or an inherent power of a state, each must be exercised within these limitations.

The language of constitutions does not mean the same thing to all people. For some, "promoting the general welfare" includes mixing of the races in public schools. For others, the "Bill of Rights" confers an absolute right to speak or to publish without responsibility. Still others interpret the First Amendment phrase about "freedom of religion" to mean sharing tax funds with sectarian groups.

The Fifth Amendment acts as a restraint upon the federal government and, by virtue of the Fourteenth, upon the states also. Government may seize private property only by adhering to the "due process" clause. The methods are by taxation, by exercise of eminent domain, and by use of reasonable police powers.

Indirect control of state schools is exercised by provisions of the Fourteenth Amendment. These prohibit legislation that would impair obligation of contracts and create second-class citizens. In

---

[7] Mayers, *The American Legal System,* p. 341.

fact, the Amendment provides the principal constitutional limitations upon the several states.

Statutory law. The second legal basis of public education is statutory law. This law, governing the relation of school personnel to pupils, to the school organization, and to society in general, is composed of state decrees and regulations promulgated by administrative officials who get authority from the legislature.

One who would understand the law as it applies to schools and education must read the statutes. Plenary power over education— authority to pass laws to carry out constitutional mandates—stems from police powers of states. It is a power which the state did not surrender when it became a member of the federal union. This power restricts private persons in order that public rights may be enhanced and protected. A state may limit the labor of school-age children, for example.

Compulsory education started more than 300 years ago. Massachusetts, in the 1640's, passed laws that required communities to establish schools. Control over education by means of state legislation thus began. Today, state statutes and administrative rules may specify the courses to be taught.[8] The state may permit school boards to adopt and enforce regulations that exclude pupils because of health reasons. They may adopt policies providing for punishment of pupils for objectionable conduct. A state law may control membership by pupils in secret societies.

Judge-made law. The third legal base of public education is the law of judges. The esteemed Justice Cardozo said that he took "judge-made law as one of the existing realities of life." Although the structure of public education stems from constitutions and statutes, the courts modify these. Some declare "judge-made" laws are best.

The "separate but equal" doctrine in public education was declared dead by the courts, not by statute. The work of deciding "what the law is" goes on every day in hundreds of courts throughout the land. These legal controversies are quarrels between two or more parties, each of whom is attempting to persuade the court of the rightfulness of his position. When a case is appealed, the courts assume (1) that any statute in question is constitutional and should be construed to preserve its validity; (2) that judicial

---

[8] See *State ex rel. Brewton* v. *Board of Education of St. Louis*, 361 Mo. 86, 233 S.W. (2d) 697 (1950), and *State Tax Commission* v. *Board of Education of Holton*, 146 Kan. 722, 73 P. (2d) 49 (1937).

power be exercised only in actual litigation and not in hypothetical cases; and (3) that the interest of the parties in the suit must be personal.

Legal jargon. Despite the fact that terms have been used throughout the first portions of this chapter in a manner that assumes understanding, it may be well to take special note of terms used regularly in legal study. These are divided into terms used (1) in connection with trials of cases, (2) in connection with case reading, and (3) pertaining to background information.

In connection with trials. A "suit" or "lawsuit" is called an action. It refers to a proceeding in a court by which one party prosecutes for the enforcement or protection of some right, the redress of a wrong, or the punishment of a public offense.[9] The statement in the formal papers filed in a court proceeding (the pleadings) is the allegation. It sets forth what the party-plaintiff expects to prove. The plaintiff brings the action and sues by filing a complaint. The defendant is the party against whom relief or recovery is sought.

A "bill" is a written complaint filed in court. The action may be "civil" (one brought to recover some right or to obtain redress for wrong done by another) or "criminal" (a proceeding instigated by government by which a party charged with a crime is brought to trial and punishment). A "demurrer" is the allegation by one party that the other party's statement (in the formal papers presented to the court) may be true but, even so, is not of such legal consequence as to justify proceeding. The "credibility of a witness" may be questioned. Here the worthiness of the testimony is in dispute. Reference may be made to the "parol-evidence rule." By this standard, oral evidence of matters not contained within a document is not admissible at the trial.

A "nonsuit" is a judgment against a plaintiff when he is unable to prove a case, or when he neglects to proceed to trial. The "judgment" is the decision of the court, usually that part involving the payment of damages.

The procedure at a trial varies, but the following steps are typical:[10]

---

[9] The explanation of these terms is based upon "Appendix B, Glossary of Legal Terms," in Madaline Kinter Remmlein, *School Law*, 2nd ed. (Danville, Ill.: The Interstate Printers and Publishers, Inc., 1962), pp. 329–336. The same list is reproduced in Rezny and Remmlein, *A Schoolman in the Law Library*, Interstate, 1962.

[10] Warren E. Gauerke, *Legal and Ethical Responsibilities of School Personnel* (Englewood Cliffs, N.J.: Prentice-Hall, Inc., 1959), pp. 7–8

1. A lawsuit results when disagreement over legal rights cannot be settled outside of court.

2. The first step is the issuance and delivery of a summons for the defendant(s) to appear before the judge at a pretrial hearing.

3. The statement of the issue by the plaintiff and the answer constitute the court pleadings.

4. In a defendant's demurrer, he temporarily admits the declaration of the plaintiff but alleges that no law makes him liable.

5. Prospective jurors may be rejected by the attorneys if their knowledge or occupation would tend to make any partial.

6. The trial is a legal process by which evidence is brought before a jury for its verdict. A trial may not have a jury, wherein the judge decides both facts and law.

7. After having testified, the witnesses are usually subjected to cross-examination to attempt to expose weaknesses in their sworn testimony.

8. The verdict entered in the court record by the trial judge becomes a judgment.

9. The carrying out of the verdict is called the execution of the judgment.

10. If errors have been committed at the original trial—in the estimation of defendant's counsel—he may appeal. When his case is accepted on appeal, it is the plaintiff who becomes the defendant.

In connection with case reading. In order to understand reported cases, the New York Regent's Prayer case will serve as a vehicle for explaining some terms.

The title of the case designates the parties, as *Steven I. Engel, et al., Petitioners,* v. *William J. Vitale, Jr., et al.* In some courts, the order is reversed on appeal when the defendant has lost and is the "Plaintiff in Error" in the court above. In the *Vitale* case there is "No. 468" as part of the case record. This is the serial number assigned when the case is filed. In *Vitale* the term and dates when the case was argued and decided are indicated as "October Term, 1961," and "June 25, 1962."

The case has a headnote which gives the rules of law laid down by the court. The court states "as many of the facts" as are necessary in understanding the decision, along with a preliminary statement of how the case came to court. The case indicates the names of counsel, and the "opinion of the court" is the explanation by the court of why it decided as it did. The "decision of the court" is what the court did in either "affirming" or "reversing" the court below.

As references to court decisions, judicial citations refer to official state reports and to the National Reporter System. Statutory citations indicate where the statute may be found in available form. Such citations include the name of the volume, the title and chapter, and the section numbers quoted.

The "majority opinion" is the statement of views of the majority in a decision in which justices disagree. In *Vitale,* Mr. Justice Black delivered the opinion. Mr. Justice Douglas rendered a "concurring opinion" because he had different reasons for arriving at the same conclusion. Mr. Justice Stewart wrote a "dissenting opinion" in which he announced his disapproval of the conclusions of the majority.

Pertaining to background information. A "writ of error" is the means whereby the appellate court orders the lower court to submit the record on which the lower court reached a judgment. This is done so that the higher court may examine the alleged errors.

Litigation may be "actions at law," which are distinguishable from those in equity. Equity is the field which differs in theory and methods of adjudication from the common law. Often, the same judges sit in the same courtrooms to preside over equity proceedings where the relief sought may be "specific performance" of a contract rather than damages awarded. The equity court seeks justice by requiring the defendant to "do the thing he promised to do." The compensation or indemnity recovered in a court of law is not the issue in equity.

If a case is not followed when the opportunity exists, that case has little legal standing. A case which has been criticized, or distinguished by subsequent cases, has little or no value. The authority of a case is completely eliminated when it has been overruled in a later case. The concept of court "jurisdiction" means that the court must not extend influence beyond its source of authority, both as to parties involved and subject matter.

"Due process" has come to be equivalent in meaning to "law of the land." It is coextensive with the doctrine of fundamental rights as used in Magna Carta. Due process of law is actually any legal proceeding in furtherance of the public good which preserves the principles of liberty and justice. The due process clause restrains all three branches of government. A correct decision is not to be considered an element of "due process of law." All that is required is a fair hearing, including the right to counsel, with opportunity to prepare a case. Any denial to an accused of a fair and impartial trial is a violation of the due process requirement, as prescribed in Amendment Six of the federal Constitution.

Some terms closely associated with the operations of school boards provide needed background information. The distinction between school districts and other corporations is that a school district possesses "restricted powers." The term often used to designate its legal status is a "quasi-municipal corporation." When applied to a school district, the phrase means an incomplete administrative unit of government. Unlike a charter for a corporation sought voluntarily from government, the school district is involuntary and imposed by the state.

A school board has the power to exercise "subjective choice" in many areas pertaining to the instructional program. Possessing "discretionary authority," a school board may delegate to its lawful agents the performance of "ministerial" duties. If a provision of law is mandatory (rather than merely directory), it must be followed strictly.

In interpreting the acts of a legislature, courts try to discover the *principle* or *purpose* of each act. They do not interfere with educational policies by substituting their judgment for that of the board of education, when those policies pertain to instruction, are reasonable, and are carried out prudently.

Where Found and How Used

Legal research is needed to find relevant background materials. A first step is to determine "what the legal question is" to which the searcher desires an answer. Apparent as this is, one may be too quick to draw conclusions as to main questions which actually confront him.

Where the law is found. After the researcher has determined this all-important legal question, the problem then is to find the answer in print. Both federal and state statutes should receive first attention. If applicable to the case—and Shepard's Citators state that they are still prevailing—these are clearly still the law.

The "source books" of law are statutes and decisions. As primary authority, they contain the law in the exact form in which it was drafted by legislative bodies or by courts. Enactments of statutes also include the law as contained in constitutions, treaties, statutes, ordinances, and administrative regulations. Decisions of the courts include those of state and federal trial courts and all appeal courts. Court decisions determine the ultimate effect of all legislative acts. Opinions of courts of record are the law where they have overturned legislative enactment.

State school laws are primary authority and create regulatory bodies and local administrative agencies. School laws may be merely general laws which authorize local school units to be specific. For information on the problems of public schools, the researcher must turn to the relevant state constitution and also to the latest published school code or session laws of the state. He should seek out publications of the United States Office of Education which contain federal and state laws and interpretations. The researcher should contact personnel of the State Department of Education for miscellaneous materials, including opinions of the attorney general.

The researcher must turn to legal encyclopedias such as *American Jurisprudence* and *Corpus Juris Secundum*. Much law is contained in law reports and reporters, and digests of the law are useful. Sometimes a start is made by using a dictionary of legal terms and phrases. Another source is called "annotations," which are selected cases with pertinent comment explaining and applying the law. General and specific books on legal problems are available. An almost encyclopedic-like series, called the "Word-Index" Approach, lists laws and cases under key words and phrases. An invaluable aid to searching in current materials is the *Index to Legal Periodicals*. To be sure that all local, state, federal, and world government publications are not overlooked, the diligent searcher must turn to *Public Affairs Information Service,* a series designed similarly to the above index.

Regardless of type, all law books not containing the sources of the law are auxiliary books. They are designed to aid in finding or clarifying the law contained in source books. These books are really "search books." The material within these books consists of statements taken from court decisions, made about such opinions, or formulated on the basis of those decisions. Usually containing numerous citations or references to the reports of judicial decisions, such books have this in common: All attempt to collect in one place under one section or heading, comments dealing with a particular legal question.

One advantage of using a "text" over the digest method is that the researcher finds material in a connected form. It enables him to make summaries of the law applicable to different situations and also provides the opportunity of explaining the relationships of decisions. The text method affords the opportunity to draw conclusions as to the law from the judicial decisions.

The "citation" includes the parties to the litigation plus volume and pages of the reports in which the decision is published. Booklets abound which illustrate and explain the function of citation books and their place in the field of legal research. To "Shepardize a case" is a common command from the senior law member to the junior partner. This means gathering citations to cases. By using Shepard's *Georgia Citations,* for example, the researcher can find all Georgia cases as cited by all Georgia and federal courts, and he can find notes of the Annotated Reports System. A specific case, one dealing with a bond validation, is cited as *Sheffield* v. *State School Building Authority et al.* It is found in Vol. 208 of the *Georgia Reports,* pp. 575–585. This case is cited in Shepard's *Georgia Citations,* February, 1953, on page 151. Here, the searcher will find the case also at 68 S.E.(2d)590. The citation to this case shows whether it was affirmed or reversed by higher courts and whether overruled, limited, questioned, or distinguished by subsequent Georgia or federal courts.

So, the researcher must use many sources to find his way through the maze of judicial decisions and laws. The great body of the law consists of precedents established by judicial decisions. The books containing decisions are "reports." Lawyers use reports and reporters to find out what the law is in a specific fact situation. Three types of reports contain decisions of the highest courts of the 50 states: (1) the Official Reports which are published for each of the states (Michigan Reports, for example); (2) the National Reporter System of the West Publishing Company (Northwestern Reporter, for example); and (3) the Annotated Reports System, published privately. The current set is the *American Law Reports* (2d series).

Three current sets of reports contain the decisions of the United States Supreme Court: (1) the U.S. *Supreme Court Reports, Single Volume Edition,* printed by the U.S. Government Printing Office; (2) the U.S. *Supreme Court Reports, Lawyers' Edition,* part of the *Annotated Reports System.* The series contains all the decisions of the Court from the time it was organized in 1789 plus certain editorial features; and (3) the *Supreme Court Reporter,* which is a unit of the National Reporter System. This series contains all decisions of the Court beginning with volume 106 of the Single Volume Edition. As in the case of the Lawyers' Edition, all decisions for one year are published in one book.

How to use school law.   To solve legal questions, the searcher uses (1) legal encyclopedias, (2) law reports, (3) textbooks and research books, (4) annotated statutes, (5) West Digest System of Key Numbers, (6) case books and law dictionaries, and (7) citators such as Shepard's.

Legal encyclopedias. The two most widely used legal encyclopedias are *American Jurisprudence* and *Corpus Juris Secundum.* Both encyclopedias (cited usually as Am. Jur. and C.J.S.) state in paragraph form what the law is. The comments used are taken from authorities cited in copious footnotes.

The topics are arranged alphabetically. Each has an analysis and subanalysis to aid the searcher to get to his problem. There are descriptive-word indexes but no table of cases. They are not legal authorities; they are persuasive regarding the issue at hand, but they are merely guides to primary authorities. Encyclopedias expound the law as it exists. They explain majority and minority opinions and relevant jurisdictional rules. Their best use is as the starting point in a search for legal questions and answers. No other source provides so confident a "frame of reference." Cases cited provide conduits "between the encyclopedia and brief paragraphs in digests which tell the searcher whether . . . he should read the entire case."[11]

The *American Jurisprudence* series provides almost complete coverage of substantive and procedural law, indicating where and when law has been modified by statute. Emphasis is placed on American law as found in the annotated reports. In the general index many words and legal maxims are listed under "Words and Phrases."

The 500 separate subjects are arranged alphabetically and kept up to date with pocket parts supplementing the index. Each volume has an index, and there is also a four-volume "General Index." Under "Schools," Vol. 47, pages 291–464, the searcher will find references to court decisions affecting the government and operation of elementary and secondary public and private schools in the United States.

The *Corpus Juris Secundum* is a complete restatement of the entire body of American law as developed by all reported cases. It makes the claim of being "the only publication which contains a textual summary of *All* the law, based on *All* the cases." The series (almost 100 separate volumes with pocket parts) includes an annotated legal dictionary and a dictionary of legal maxims as

---

[11] Miles O. Price and Harry Bitner, *Effective Legal Research* (Englewood Cliffs, N.J.: Prentice-Hall, Inc., 1953), p. 174.

well. A single alphabet provides the arrangement for each of the several hundred fields of law—from "Actions" to "Wills." For example, the field of "Schools and School Districts" appears in volumes 78 and 79, with a detailed outline at the front of this broad topic and a complete index following it.

Law reports. School law is basically found in court decisions. A bare statute does not constitute the law, rather, it is the judicial interpretation which is law. One must look to the decisions—to collections of published "reports" for these. Most books in the law library are the means of unlocking the "mountain of rules" found in reports. A law report may be defined as

> . . . the production of an adequate record of a judicial decision on a point of law, in a case heard in open court, for the subsequent citation as a precedent. A law report is a report of law, and not of fact. Only the issues and the facts relevant to the point of law should be recorded, since every judgment is founded on a situation of fact.[12]

In such a report the law expounded may be an interpretation of a portion of a constitution, or part of a statute; it may be an application of a principle of the common law. From these "reports" —which are decisions of the highest courts—knowledge is derived of unwritten law (as opposed to the consciously formulated law of legislative bodies).

In 1876, John B. West and Company published "The Syllabi" which grew into the *National Reporter System.* Shortly thereafter, the pamphlet became the *North Western Reporter.* In it appeared the current supreme court decisions of five Midwestern states and one territory. One Reporter after another was added. By 1887, the United States was covered by a series of seven Reporters—now all units of the National Reporter System. These Reporters currently give in full all appellate court decisions in the United States.

Selected reporters provide needed material in accurate form about cases outside the 50 state court systems. The *Supreme Court Reporter* contains each decision of the Supreme Court of the United States. The *Federal Reporter* includes cases from the United States Court of Appeals from its founding in 1891. The *Federal Supplement* reports decisions of the United States District Courts.

By using the reporters, the searcher can look up decisions of any state; he will find title, court term and dates, headnote or syllabus, statement of the facts, and opinion of the court.

---

[12] *Ibid,* p. 93.

Law digests. A digest is a book of index which catalogs cases decided by courts in a digest-paragraph rather than outline or text style. A subject index to the rules of law raised or discussed in reported cases, it has no logical arrangement, since decisions are published in chronological order.

The digest-paragraph is a succinct statement of the facts of a case with principles of law which the court applied. Two types are in general use, one a full paragraph digest and the other a short-line digest. The preparation of either is important and tells much about the complexity of the law. First, the digest-maker composes a separate statement for each question or point of law decided in each case to be digested. Second, he classifies these statements under various titles and subdivisions.

The digest is the principal method of presenting legal material. The *Federal Digest* includes all cases. One of numerous components is the *United States Supreme Court Digest,* covering all decisions of the Court from its start to date.

The *American Digest System* covers all printed opinion from every American jurisdiction since 1685. Called the "master set" of all digests, each of the eight units has a complete index of reported cases during the period of time covered by that unit.

Digests are formidable in appearance but contain indexes, the most widely used being the West Key Number. All five digests— the *American Digest System, United States Supreme Court Digest, Federal Digest, Reporter Digests,* and *State Digests*—employ the key-number plan. One permanent key number exists for every legal proposition, with each point of law assigned a topic and key number. The sole obstacle facing the researcher is locating that "key" for the proposition he is investigating. The key-number classification breaks the body of the law into 421 topics. All cases involving one point are thus brought together for study.

Textbooks and related works. This division of legal materials includes textbooks, monographs, commentaries, and histories. An example of a textbook is Prosser's text on *Torts,* presenting legal material in a connected manner as statements of principles and rules of law. Textbooks are intended for instruction or as case finders. They include bar review books, treatises on a single subject, and law books for the layman.

The *Restatements of the Law* come under the heading of textbooks or commentaries. These cover many fields, such as contracts, torts, and trusts. Professors of law composed the *Restatements,* issued by the American Law Institute. In deciding cases, judges often cite the *Restatements*. They tend to unify interpretations of the common law.

Annotated legal materials. State and federal governments maintain a compilation of laws arranged by subject, regardless of date of enactment. Various federal statute books containing the United States Constitution have explanatory and critical notes on the subject matter, and each paragraph, sentence, phrase, or word is "annotated" or commented upon. A fully annotated edition of the Constitution of the United States cites not only all the United States Supreme Court cases in point, but also those of state courts. An annotation of the "particular point in question" cites opinions of the Attorney General of the United States, Presidential executive orders and proclamations, and pertinent law review articles.

Federal statutes appear in annotated editions. The *United States Code* has the convenience of laws organized by titles with explanatory notes. The Code draws upon the *Statutes at Large* which take legal precedence.

The search for answers to legal problems by means of annotated materials involves a combination of digest and text methods. An excellent example is found in the *American Law Reports*. Each annotation is a complete discussion of a particular legal question, and each contains citations to all cases in which both state and federal courts have decided that question. The annotation indicates the holding and distinctive features of each of the cases.

There are annotated editions of state statutes, with some being annotated codes. Here, laws are arranged by topics rather than chronologically, with future alterations indicated, whether by the legislature, administrative bodies, or the courts.

Periodicals and law dictionaries. Like those in most disciplines, legal periodicals are of many kinds. One of the most useful and respected is the law school review. These are published by law schools, and each issue includes book reviews, special features, recent cases, notes, and comments—all in addition to feature articles.

To aid the searcher in getting at materials in periodicals, a most useful tool is the *Index to Legal Periodicals*. The arrangement is by alphabet under a plan based upon the West's American Digest System. There are interim supplements to keep the searcher currently abreast.

A dictionary of legal terms is needed to note exact meanings.

Foreign words as well as English words are often included. Good dictionaries will provide a table of abbreviations also.

Citators. A citation book or "citator" aids the researcher in finding out what has happened to a statute or any portion of the federal or state constitutions. Constitutions are amended—as are statutes—by change, repeal, and court interpretation. Citators reveal this information, and no other single research tool does. One knows whether a case is still good authority for a point of law stated in the first paragraph of the syllabus. One can determine whether the case has been commented upon in legal periodicals or mentioned in annotations.

Shepard's Citations are considered to be the most complete citator system. By using *Shepard's Citations to Statutes,* for example, the lawyer discovers every instance where a particular section of a statute has been affected by subsequent legislation, and where that section of the statute has been cited, applied, or construed by the courts. The use of *Shepard's Citations* (federal and state) quickly determines the present-day value of authorities upon which the searcher may plan to rely as evidence of the law in a case.

Some Typical Kinds of Problems

School law covers a wide variety of problems, and "typical" examples will illustrate this scope. Types of problems are identified below under broad headings, with a case illustrating the school law issue.

School board policy. More than 30,000 boards of education must reach decisions involving elections, legality of bids, interpretations of operating rules, meetings and procedures, Bible reading, secret societies, health regulations, "flag salute," school assignment, and transportation.

Religious freedom. Perhaps no issue generates so much emotion as the "Church-State" question. The reciting of prayers in public schools has divided some communities. During the October 1961 term of the United States Supreme Court, Mr. Justice Black delivered the opinion in the "prayer case."[13] Here, the respondent Board of Education (of Union Free School District No. 9, New Hyde Park, New York) acted in its official capacity under

---

[13] *Engel et al.* v. *Vitale, Jr., et al.,* 370 U.S. 421. Case was actually dated June 25, 1962, at the close of the 1961–62 term.

state law to direct the school district's principal to cause a prayer to be said aloud by each class in the presence of a teacher at the start of each school day. The board had adopted the procedure on recommendation of the Board of Regents, a governmental agency created by the state constitution, and one to which the legislature had granted broad powers over the public school system. Officials of the state composed the prayer and had it published as a part of their "Statement on Moral and Spiritual Training in the Schools." Parents of public school pupils brought legal action, insisting that use of this official prayer was contrary to beliefs of themselves and their children. They challenged the legality of both the state law authorizing use of the prayer and the regulation ordering recitation on the ground that such actions by governmental agencies violated part of the First Amendment of the federal Constitution.

In its decision, the United States Supreme Court made one point: This was a religious activity. By using its public school system to encourage recitation of the Regents' prayer, the State of New York had adopted a practice "wholly inconsistent with the Establishment Clause." Government had not remained "neutral."

School attendance. This topic embraces such divergent subjects as the Church-State issue of released-time and shared-time programs, nature of legal residence, truancy, age, handicaps as bars to attendance, married pupils, home instruction, vaccination, and segregation of races.

The married pupil. School administrators become concerned when marriage involves pupils of compulsory school age. May they legally exclude a married woman from school if she desires to attend and continue her studies? May they compel the married pupil to attend if he is under the legal quitting age?

Married people are considered to be outside the attendance laws even though they may be within compulsory school attendance age. However, every child has a constitutional and statutory right to attend school, provided his moral standards are not objectionable. It is the policy of government to encourage pupils to equip themselves with a good education, and rules excluding married pupils from attendance are successfully challenged as being unreasonable.[14]

Contractual obligations. The notion of "offer and acceptance"

---

[14] This rule was stated by the Supreme Court of Louisiana, *re State in Interest of Goodwin,* 214 La. 1062, 39 So. (2d) 731 (decided in 1949). All courts support the proposition that marriage alone is not legal ground for denying a child attendance at school.

is basic to all mutual agreements. Contract law includes such subjects as requirement for competitive bidding, whether employment agreements must be in writing, nepotism, conflict of interests, teachers' unions and the right to strike, and duties under contract.

Right to strike.   Whether school employees have a right to strike for what their association deems desirable ends was the issue in the case of the Norwalk Teachers' Association.[15] A dispute arose over salary between the board and an independent labor union representing almost all the teachers. After negotiations, about two-thirds of the teacher members rejected contracts offered them and refused to return to teaching duties. The press called the action a "strike." The court granted a declaratory judgment, stating rights of the parties. The Court of Errors of Connecticut stated that strikes by school employees were illegal, but found it legal for teachers to organize as a labor union. It could not engage in concerted action, such as a strike, work stoppage, or collective refusal to perform their contractual duties.

Nonpublic schools.   Many questions involving the status of nonpublic schools are litigated. These pertain to the authority to transport nonpublic school pupils at public cost; released and shared-time plans; legal definition of a parochial school; state laws requiring public school attendance; ordinances which discriminate between public and private schools; and the wearing of distinctive religious garb in public schools.

Authority to operate.   A case quoted frequently as an example of religious freedom and the right of a parent to send his child to a school where religion is a part of the curriculum is the "Society of Sisters" case from Oregon.[16] Sisters who operated parochial schools and owners of a military school sought to restrain enforcement of a state law requiring children to attend public schools exclusively. The Supreme Court of the United States held that no state has authority to require attendance at public schools only, and that such a compulsory law was a violation of the "due-process clause" of the Fourteenth Amendment.

School finances.   The question of money seems to lie at the core of many controversies involving schools. Revenue is a part of the issue when a state taxes federal property. Diverting funds from one

---

[15] *Norwalk Teachers' Association* v. *Board of Education,* 138 Conn. 269, 83 A. (2d) 482 (1951).

[16] *Pierce* v. *Society of Sisters; Pierce* v. *Hill Academy,* 268 U.S. 510 (1925). Cited also in 45 S. Ct. 571, 69 L. Ed. 1070, and 39 A.L.R. 468.

purpose to another, control of educational policy through control of funds, use of special nontax school funds, legality of charging fees in public schools, illegal taxation, and school district debt limits all revolve around money.

Diversion of school funds. When a board of education is pressed for funds, it may attempt to use school dollars for a purpose for which it was not designated. The right of a board to purchase a farm was challenged in California.[17] Under authority of the School Code, which permitted issuance of bonds to purchase school lots, people in the district voted bonds to raise money for a number of projects, including a school laboratory farm. The clerk of the county refused to sign the bonds because the voters, under the law as written, had no legal power to vote the bonds. The District Court of Appeal agreed that the authority to vote the bonds to finance purchase of lots could not include farms.

Personnel concerns. The topic of personnel concerns includes the traditional "welfare issues." As such, the topic deals with seniority problems for promotion purposes, social security payments in lieu of retirement programs, probationary status, certificates needed for teaching, insurance programs, tenure rights, leaves of absence, dismissal from position, oaths of allegiance, and academic freedom.

Teacher oaths. In New York State the Feinberg law was passed in the early 1950's to rid state schools of subversive teachers. Pursuant to that law, elaborate machinery was set up to implement the provisions. Reports on each school employee were required. Enforcement had been in abeyance, pending suit to test its constitutionality.

In the famous *Adler case,* the United States Supreme Court held that the law did not violate the right of free speech and that it did not deprive teachers of liberty without due process.[18] The presumption was sustained that membership in a subversive organization means allegiance, and that a teacher could declare under oath that he rebutted such presumption. In dissenting opinions, two Justices of a divided court stated that the law rested on the belief that government should limit the flow of ideas into men's minds. Even more critical, Justice Douglas found it impossible to accept the doctrine

---

17 *Board of Supervisors of Merced County* v. *Cothran,* 84 Cal. App. (2d) 679, 191 P. (2d) 506 (1948).

18 *Adler* v. *Board of Education of City of New York,* 342 U.S. 485, 72 S. Ct. 215 (1952).

that one who entered public service could be forced to sacrifice his civil rights. He said the law was destructive of an indispensable privilege of the teacher—academic freedom.

School facilities. The use of school buildings for nonschool purposes is a problem in many communities. Insurance coverage is a concern. Joint construction of school buildings and use by two districts pose other dilemmas. An issue is the control and location by local ordinances of buildings used for school purposes.

Nonschool use. A New York case illustrates dangers in the use of schools by outside groups. In Yonkers, the board refused to permit use of one of its school buildings by the "Committee for Peace" group.[19] A school law granted authority to permit the use of school buildings "for holding social, civic and recreational meetings and entertainments, and other uses pertaining to the welfare of the community. . . ." Regularly, New York public schools were used for civic forums and as community centers.

In the *Ellis* case, the board gave no reason for denying use of the building to the Committee for Peace. As the plaintiff, the Committee insisted that in failing to state a reason the board was discriminating against the group. The case went to the courts on grounds of denial of "equal protection of the laws" under the First and Fourteenth Amendments. By a 5 to 4 decision, the United States Supreme Court sustained the board's action. Refusing to consider the case, the Court stated that boards may make reasonable classifications of organizations which will be permitted to use school property.

Torts. Within this single category of law fall most school cases. Topics include (1) personal liability of employees and of board members for injury; (2) defamation of character; (3) use by teachers of personal automobiles to transport pupils off school grounds; (4) school safety patrols; (5) corporal punishment; (6) "trips to Washington" and other field excursions; (7) building hazards; (8) playground nuisances; (9) injuries to spectators at school-sponsored, out-of-class events; and (10) school bus accidents.

Defamation of character. Since a tort is a legal wrong, the act may be intentional, such as harming a person's reputation. A plaintiff may allege that a defendant injured her professionally as

---

[19] *Ellis* v. *Dixon,* 349 U.S. 458, 75 S. Ct. 850 (1955); and 118 N.Y.S. (2d) 815 (1953). The Supreme Court of New York is a trial court, not an appellate one.

a teacher and bring an action for slander (spoken defamation).[20] The teacher may allege that the defendant made a false report to school board members about her having a contagious disease. She may be dismissed and unable to obtain any position as teacher. The defendant could deny charges and not set up the affirmative defense of privileged communication.

A court might say that a false report of one's profession was actionable *per se* (in and of itself) unless the defendant showed it was made under privilege. Every repetition of a slander originated by a third person could be held a new publication (whether oral or written). Statements made to board members would be privileged, but not those made to other citizens. To establish privilege, the talebearer must be motivated by right intent and speak only to those who have a legitimate concern with the subject.

School district powers.   Where community conflict exists, it is difficult not to permit such conflict to be aired in public. Topics of debate might be school building corporations, elections, property damages, reorganization plans, changes in territorial boundaries, annexations, legal boundaries, or debt limits.

Authority to maintain a high school.   A railway company with others challenged the legality of a school district levy to maintain a high school.[21] The grounds were that the school district had no authority to maintain a high school. The court made it clear that boards have powers to establish schools of different grades, to adopt regulations for admission of pupils, and to assign pupils. The court said that high schools were not prohibited by law and that a school district could do more than what the law required.[22]

Court Systems in the United States

The average citizen would probably readily admit that he would fail a test on the Bill of Rights. His knowledge of the American legal system, too, is fragmentary. Even a well-informed person faces a baffling task when he seeks a clear picture of legal institutions.[23]

---

[20] *Brown* v. *McCann,* 36 Ga. App. 812, 138 S. E. 247 (Georgia, 1927). This subject may be found in 33 *American Jurisprudence,* "Libel and Slander" secs. 46, 131. See also 58 A.L.R. 1165 and subsequent annotations. In the *American Digest System,* "Libel and Slander" has the Key No. 9(5).

[21] *People* v. *Chicago and North Western Railway Co.,* 122 N.E. (2d) 527 (Illinois, 1954).

[22] The early landmark case about creating high schools without express legislative authority was decided affirmatively in the last century. *Stuart* v. *School District No. 1 of Kalamazoo,* 30 Mich. 69 (1874).

[23] Mayers, *The American Legal System,* p. vii.

A multiplicity of laws and courts and jurisdictions makes up a legal maze.

That part of government called "the legal system" is concerned with proceedings through which a variety of tribunals adjudicate rights of individuals and society. These tribunals are armed with the power of government.

The system of federal courts. As a federal union composed of 50 political communities, the United States has two court systems. The dual plan stems directly from a separate judicial power, created by the federal Constitution. Only in the District of Columbia, the territories, and the insular possessions of the United States is there but one system.

The federal court structure is made up of the United States Supreme Court, United States (Circuit) Courts of Appeal, United States District Courts, and specialized courts. These federal courts sit side by side with state courts, but they function in almost complete isolation. State courts respond to the Supreme Court of the United States by means of intermediate appellate courts. Except for a minority of cases finally passed upon by the United States Supreme Court, all such appeals are disposed of by regional appellate courts.

For appeals from district courts, the United States is divided into ten "circuits." In each sits a United States Court of Appeals. Territories and insular possessions are included within the ten regions, but the District of Columbia constitutes a separate one.

The United States District Courts form the base of the federal judiciary and have original jurisdiction only; they can hear cases not decided by other courts. Courts of Appeal have appellate jurisdiction only; they can hear cases appealed from lower federal courts.

The United States Supreme Court. "The most dazzling jewel in the judicial crown of the United States is the revered, august, and powerful United States Supreme Court."[24] The Court rarely exercises its limited original jurisdiction. Appellate jurisdiction over lower federal courts is achieved by means of a few hundred selected cases per year. In a smaller number of cases the Court reviews—as to federal questions only—decisions of state courts. Unique among courts of the land, it brings together into one strand threads from diverse pieces of the judicial fabric.

---

[24] Henry J. Abraham, *Courts and Judges* (New York: Oxford University Press, 1959), p. 22.

About 1500 cases per year (out of some 50,000 that come to over 90 federal district courts) are appealed to the Supreme Court. Of the 1500, approximately 200 are handled, from which the Court issues opinions on only 80 to 100. Through these, the United States Supreme Court interprets the language of the federal Constitution and serves as the final arbiter as to whether a person has been deprived of his liberty or property. If as many as four justices desire to review a case, a petition for a "writ of certiorari" is granted. The Court itself issues the writ directly to the court below, commanding it to certify a record of the case.

Central to an understanding of federal judicial power is the fact that the three corresponding departments of the national government are *not* parallel and coordinate at all. The legislature and the executive branches are brought into being by the Constitution itself. Not so the judiciary! It had no existence until Congress and the President had acted. In fact, the High Court was a creation of the Congress, not of the Constitution.[25]

The doctrine of states' rights. Neither private nor public opinion as to the desirability of an order of a federal court provides any legal basis for delaying a prompt start toward compliance. Education is not mentioned in seven main articles within the body of the Constitution. The Tenth Amendment reserves to the states all powers not delegated to the federal government. Under this Amendment, education is a province reserved to the states, but it must be conducted in accordance with federal law. To the humiliation of some citizens since 1954, the fact of this doctrine has been proved.

The doctrine of judicial review. Much of the actual work of the United States Supreme Court is concerned with the constitutionality of both state and federal laws. If at least five of the nine justices find that a statute is contrary to "what that majority then believes the Constitution to say," that law is declared invalid. It is struck down and has no force as of that moment. This procedure and result is known as "judicial review of legislative acts."

The United States Supreme Court has repeatedly said that unconstitutionality of a law must be read as meaning illegality under the federal Constitution. The Constitution itself is the source of the right to bring action to enjoin the enforcement of a federal law that is felt to be repugnant to that document. It also created the

---

[25] This is just one of many illuminating points brought out by Mayers in his book, *The American Legal System,* Chapter One.

right to enjoin the enforcement of any state constitutional provision or statute which runs counter to the "supreme law of the land."

One consequence of the judiciary's acting after the legislative branch is that in particular cases it is in the position to make its view of the Constitution prevail. Perhaps more important, the courts are influential in determining future readings of the Constitution by the other two branches. In determining legality of acts of legislatures, "judicial review" modifies party government and necessitates bipartisan cooperation or a "combination" to amend the Constitution.

The Judiciary Act.   Federal courts have jurisdiction of all cases arising under the United States Constitution and federal laws. In 1789, each state ceased to be a sovereignty, subjecting itself to the superior power of the Constitution and national government. The First Congress enacted the "Judiciary Act of 1789," creating "one Supreme Court" and a system of inferior federal courts.

In the Judiciary Act, Congress conferred upon inferior federal courts original jurisdiction over many classes of cases enumerated in the Constitution. In addition, it provided for the composition of the Supreme Court and for a division of the nation into 13 districts.

Jurisdiction, not judicial power.   A case falling within the judicial power of the United States may be within the jurisdiction of several federal courts, depending upon the statute governing that court. All cases to which a state is a party must come within the jurisdiction of the Supreme Court. The jurisdiction of federal courts is independent but concurrent with that of state courts.

Judges have maintained that there is a fundamental difference between "jurisdiction" and "judicial power." The distinction is that a lower federal court has no jurisdiction except where Congress has specifically given it. Once a court has jurisdiction of a case, it is thereby put in possession of the power to decide the case. The United States Supreme Court will not take jurisdiction of a case when it should not do so. It must, however, exercise its jurisdiction when it should do so.

System of state courts.   An almost self-sufficient system of courts functions in each of the 50 states. Each exhibits such diversity as to make any general comment meaningless. Courts of original jurisdiction are trial courts despite the fact that proceedings may involve no trials at all. In appellate courts, decisions of lower courts are affirmed, modified, or set aside. In most state courts, jurisdiction is either exclusively original or solely appellate.

"Judicial power" was entrusted to state courts in considerable measure from the beginning of the Republic. Congress provided that cases started in state courts should remain there. They proceed through the highest state court, and then only may review of a federal question be sought.

Law and equity courts. The legal framework just described took a long time to develop. In this process substantial tradition accumulated. Out of it came "law courts" and "courts of equity." These are distinct courts, even though the same courtroom and same judge are used for both proceedings.

Four types of court actions are mentioned here as illustrative of the differences in subject matter. The first three are actions in law. The last is a writ from an equity court. (1) Mandamus is an order from a law court compelling some action by a public officer or body. (2) A second writ is that of prohibition, used to restrict or stop altogether any action on a matter outside the jurisdiction of the person or body to which the writ is directed. (3) "Quo warranto" is a legal writ used to try title to a public office. (4) "Injunction" is an order of a court of equity—which may be temporary or permanent—requiring the party enjoined to refrain from a specific action.

The last action is equity because courts here act on the person of the defendant rather than against his property. Equity grew up outside the legal framework to supply a different approach to the problem of governing men.

CHAPTER III

Organization of American
Public Education

Good schools cannot be maintained on "good will and senti-
mental feelings" alone, or on pure legal bases either. The American
people generally believe that public schools must be organized
and operated to serve the interests of all children. They feel that
schools have a necessary contribution to make to the development
of an American way of life. Thus, provisions are made for schools
which are supported by tax funds and which are available to all
who can profit from them. As practical persons who pay taxes, citizens should know about the relation between educational organization and school law.

It is usual to hear such comment as, "Why doesn't the P.T.A.
do something about getting us good teachers? All they do is talk."
The remark comes from one who forgets that the P.T.A. is a voluntary group, extra-legal, and has no business involving itself in employment of personnel. Parents and the Association are not in
the chain of command and must function outside the hierarchy.
Only as "people" do parents choose their elected leaders. With the
help of the school superintendent, board members (acting as the
board) make such decisions.

Sometimes the interest of educators in securing improved organization clashes with legal obstacles. In many states, legal obstacles are formidable. In pressing for improvements, educators
may run into statutes which make school district reorganization
"almost impossible." Because of tightened school budgets (other
governmental units require increased spending also), school services
are sometimes curtailed. Longer periods and more subjects are
being tried in some places in answer to the charge of not being
"tough enough" in the curriculum. A timely question is: What are
desirable organizational, structural, and operational policies needed
to facilitate learning?

Many people pin labels on parts of programs to call attention to
"defects" as the label-pinners see them. Regardless of these tags,
thinking persons continue to be concerned about the culturally

disadvantaged youngster. He does not fit into present organizational patterns. Some educators describe him as "indifferent to responsibilities, of low social status, exhibiting poor classroom response, having marked physical defects, practicing bad habits, showing unacceptable behaviors, possessing limited aspiration, and demonstrating inferior achievement, due in part to poor attendance and then final dropout from school altogether."

Reasons for Organization

In pioneer days, the Midwest made few attempts at organizing classes, much less whole schools or districts. Often as not, the "whole school of eight" recited en masse. Every teacher created his own curriculum, which varied from year to year. The McGuffey Readers were the most important series of teaching aids. These were widely distributed, especially in the country schools.

Today, however, all is different. There are questions about whether the board should organize for "team teaching," for a "modified core," or adopt the "ungraded primary" plan. Questioners wonder whether (1) junior colleges ought to be part of the present secondary school, (2) whether vocational education at its best is not truly liberalizing, or (3) why an intermediate school district is not best for school organization in the Midwest as well as the South.

The law helps little to find answers, but it affects decisions very much. Research has thrown much light on annoying problems of organization which have plagued people for so long. Should boards create centralized or decentralized systems? Should there be the pyramidal or flat structure? Must there be the "line and staff" organization? What is *the* best span of control for the executive? Where should the center of authority lie for best results? What is the optimum size of school districts? What should be the relation of the educational enterprise to government? Law may hinder when people wish to alter traditional patterns. Constitutions and laws are sometimes at odds with insights of theoreticians and with current public thought.

In an analysis of structures for educational policy-making, one is confronted with the fact that public education is almost endlessly organized. People want something from government. They organize, building a coalition of influence to attempt to get that something. Others, opposed to "that something," build a coalition to block possible action. Thus, there are numerous organizations. There is the education association, the teachers union, and the various associations for principals, superintendents, guidance counselors, classroom teachers, vocational education specialists, and coaches. Officials of these groups do not act in concert. In the proliferation of groups, there are clashes.

Interested persons get into the P.T.A., Council for Better Schools, the Association for University Women, the League for Women Voters, Federation of Women's Clubs, Women's Legislative Councils, and Associations for Mental Health and the Mentally Retarded. Here they seek to support education on the broad front—to secure "their brand of enlightened leadership." In any discussion about "whither education," a casual listener may hear talk about the "increase in federal control of education." He may hear that "too many federal laws and court decisions" are changing time-honored patterns.

The nation can ill afford to retain outmoded and ineffective forms of organization when new knowledge often demands radical changes. Laws which support outworn patterns can be altered more effectively when the over-all structure of American public education is understood. The public must be helped to realize that in the mid-1960's there are fewer than 35,000 separate school districts, compared to more than 100,000 before World War II. Laws, however, still hamper the achieving of other alterations in educational structures. Perhaps the courts have given us, for too long a time, a feeling of well-being which has kept us from correcting basic defects. Some believe that Americans have tended to lean too heavily on the courts instead of correcting the legal structure by means of legislation.

Appropriate Educational Jargon

How people behave within organization is not always reflected in attainment of stated goals. The activities of an organization (be it a lodge, church, or government) should be related to purposes —ideas expressed in words. Words are often misunderstood, however.

Texts in school administration must refer to organization and administration in terms of symbols—words, charts, and numerals. Authors talk about "decision-making becoming recognized as the heart of organization" and the "process of administration." Some state that choice properly evolves from a consideration of its probable consequences when it is acted upon, not from fixed principles.

The "process of administration" eludes description. The power structure in a public school system can, of course, be detected by using more words. It is an unequal distribution of authority, and it involves force, domination, and manipulation.

When attention is drawn away from "power structure" to other terms, the task gets no easier. Organization of a school program involves planning, guidance of personnel, and management of time and facilities. The law may define "the required courses to be studied," but it provides no guide to understanding people and their behavior.

To avoid further confusion, it is proposed to explain the following terms used in speaking about organization: "administration," "organization," "policy" and "procedure," "hierarchy," and some miscellaneous terms known as "POSDCoRB."

Administration. The purpose of administration is to "run things" and to "get things done." *The* administration of any organization must employ personnel and must organize the staff so that communication is established within and outside the organization. Rules and programs of action must be formulated. Administration uses materiel, must provide funds, must provide for evaluation of its outcomes, and must interpret results to its own public. Educational administration does all these things by using budgets and business methods, by adopting pupil and staff personnel policies, by providing school plant facilities, and by making available special services to those who require them.

Traditionally, administration has achieved its purposes by issuing orders or directives. These cannot violate legal bounds but can vary greatly. Administration determines policy below the legislative branch of government and is the application of tried techniques, such as sound organization, capable personnel, and adequate planning. It is the achievement of purpose and it employs all of these.

Organization. The means through which administration acts is called organization. The machinery is set up by administration with defined channels through which operations should proceed. Organization of effort results from coordination of parts to relate each to common purposes.

Whenever two or more persons combine efforts in a definite manner for a given purpose, organization is present. They have ordered their behavior to perform certain tasks to accomplish goals. Organization refers, though, to more than this framework for operation; it is more than any visible edifice. It is the collection of persons systematically arranged, including the functions and coordination of activities as each relates to common tasks.

In addition to legal proscriptions, organization itself limits accomplishment of objectives. There are many ways of organizing a thousand persons into a cooperating unit—all within legal bounds. In some large city school systems, organization provides for lesser units within the district—sometimes up to eight or ten. These customarily bear such labels as instruction, personnel, research, service clinics, child accounting, supplies, finance, and plant (broken down into operations, maintenance, extension, and auditing).

Sometimes "bureaucracy" is used to refer to the "overorganized" school, industry, or state. Researchers have developed information and communication theories to aid in better understanding of bigness. From such studies it seems clear that organization is but one of the many kinds of communication.

Law takes no account of whether persons in an organization agree or disagree with the administrative directives or purposes. Results, however, may be totally different in terms of output. Law makes no allowance for the effect on organization from participation of teachers in policy-making and administration of school systems. No law provides for the informal organization which develops within groups, despite the legal authority which status persons possess. Persons in the formal organization have their parallel roles in the informal structures, but power relationships and communication channels are often strikingly different.

Policy.   This can be a statement of intentions or a stated course of conduct. It is a reflection of the philosophy of the power group. Statements of policy are made on critical issues and are designed to resolve these issues. School board policy is board philosophy— whether it be budget figures or words.

Policy is a statement of a rule or principle which the board agrees should be followed in deciding types of cases or problems. It is the rationale by which it should operate the schools. The curriculum is one aspect of policy—perhaps the most vital—which the superintendent is charged with carrying out. School-sponsored activities reflect the educational policy of the voters, who select the board which makes the curriculum one source of legal authority.

Procedure.   This describes a uniform manner for carrying out an operation, usually based on policy previously established. A board might state that children of the school district above grade three are to remain on the school campus during the noon hour. The details of the program for each school, worked out to suit it, are the procedures. Documentation of policies and procedures usually are written statements, adopted by the board and developed by the administrator of the school.

Educational Hierarchy. This is the scalar aspect of a public school system within a state. The term indicates that a series of positions exists in order of authority from the top to bottom. Some are created by law, while others are not. Where straight line-staff delegation is found, authority within a school system is from the board of education to the superintendent, to his assistants, to the building principals, and then to the teachers. Within a state system, the hierarchy is made up of a state board of education, which gets authority from the statutes. The legislature creates administrative agencies. These and their agents may pass rules and regulations. If consistent with law, each has the authority of law in controlling the operation of schools within the school districts of the state.

In the educational hierarchy, parents and the courts are of necessity omitted. Parents are in the line of authority as "people," each parent affecting education by choosing or rejecting the state constitution or law makers. The courts function outside of the hierarchy because they are brought into operation by persons or agencies within the line. A teacher may become a plaintiff by instigating a court action. A principal may file suit against a board for breach of contract. Only then does the court appealed to step in the line "to do justice."

The line personnel have immediate responsibility for carrying out the instructional program, as authorized by law. Those who are identified as "staff personnel" possess responsibility for providing services, facilities, and materials needed to carry out the program of instruction. In charting authority and responsibility, line personnel appear in the vertical structure, with positions indicated by solid lines. The staff or service personnel are only assistants to line personnel, with relationships shown by broken lines. They may recommend only. None has legal authority to effect action on his own.

Persons employed within a school building are members of the staff—instructional and noninstructional. All are staff members, whether or not they possess "line" authority. Think of "staff personnel" as service workers not possessing administrative authority. Then, a teacher's legal authority over a pupil will be seen as "line" despite his being a "staff" member.

Functions of boards may be "mixed," depending upon circumstances. An administrative board, such as those operating public schools, may possess functions other than policy-making. For example, a board is quasi-judicial when it sits at a dismissal hearing of an employee. It performs "judging" functions as well as "rule-making" ones.

Miscellaneous terms. These pertain to organization and come from the Gulick grid, known as "POSDCoRB." Any organization is better comprehended by a grasp of these related concepts.

Planning. This is the first element of the grid. Planning embraces policy, program, and staffing. It permits unity of operation, continuity, flexibility, and precision of effort. Involved in planning are such activities as investigation, evaluation, forecast, and the determination of action. In short, planning is needed to establish machinery for achieving objectives. It is affected by the legal structure and limits of desirable social policy.

Planning recognizes these controls: It is a prelude to providing for funds, evaluation, and interpretation. Planning assures that all will be done in accordance with rules laid down and instructions given. Control in organization is the exertion of power to manage behavior of persons within the organization to carry out plans.

Organizing. This is the second element and should require no further explanation. Staffing is the third element. Directing is often used synonymously with control. Coordinating is a synonym for systematizing and harmonizing effort within organization. The reporting function deals with interpretation of effort to persons within the organization and to persons outside. Budgeting is the last of the seven elements. The term narrowly refers to apportioning anticipated income over a given period, in advance of spending. More broadly, budgeting means the planned use of human energy, physical facilities, and time so that goals can be accomplished well and with a minimum of effort. As a plan for use of resources, a budget reflects the philosophy of an organization better than do words submitted in annual reports.

Within the grid are related terms which have come to be precise. Administrative authority within organization refers to the right to require action of others—the permission of a subordinate to have his behavior influenced by a superior without independently examining merits of the decision. With authority, there should be commensurate responsibility—accountability for performance of duties.

For any work to be accomplished, communication processes are vital. Individuals are influenced by verbal and nonverbal means, an essential feature of which is that the receiver "gets the message" in the manner or form intended. A blow on the head is communication. However, within an organization, more civilized and less obvious devices must be employed. At times, silence itself may communicate much.

Organizations function by means of delegation. One accomplishes through the agency of another that which one is empowered to do himself. The delegator invests one person (or group) with the power to act for himself. In this temporary sharing of power, a line person delegates administrative authority. He should then see that responsibility is commensurate.

Leadership is another nonlegal concept. Law makes no provision for this elusive but necessary ingredient within organization. It embraces both stimulation and "command" elements. A true leader inspires confidence, causing persons to think and then behave in the ways he wants them to act. The leader of an organization (and those who lead under his delegated authority) must strive for unity, seeing that actions are taken which point to unified purposes. Unity of command assures that each member of the team receives direction from one person. Unity of management requires that there be but one plan of operation, with singleness of purpose emphasizing that there be but one or several nonconflicting purposes.

The jargon of organization makes sense if it is used when and where it should be used. Direction provides for the formulation of general policy. Administration is the conduct of the enterprise within the framework of direction. Management pertains to the detailed conduct of things.

State Organization for Public Education

A majority of the 50 states has administrative organizations for public education which involve two levels of policy-making responsibility: state and local. Within this framework are the legal bases for American public education—constitutions of the 50 states, bodies of school laws, and decisions of appellate courts.

Fundamental to an understanding of legal principles and organization of public education in the United States is a realization that the public school is part of government. The Tenth Amendment leaves authority and responsibility to organize any system the states deem appropriate. The public schools, therefore, are creatures of state legislatures. They have plenary (almost complete) power over education, except as modified by constitutional restraints (both state and federal). State legislatures do have a choice as to how to exercise their powers and can be brought before superior tribunals to answer for failures to act.

Education in no part belongs to local government. Taxes collected locally for schools are state funds, and teachers employed locally in public schools by school districts are state employees, carrying out state business.

Each time a legislature meets, new laws are passed which directly affect education within the state. Some statutes affecting public school programs are spelled out in detail, with all foreseeable contingencies accounted for. In others, only broad powers are mentioned, with details left to other state agencies.

Because of the plenary power of the state over education, legislatures have authority to alter school districts. They may dissolve them without getting permission from electors. The state provides for changes of school districts by means of dissolution, consolidation, or annexation.

The state board of education gets authority from provisions of the statutes and in the state constitution, which may make provision for a chief state school officer. The board exercises general control over elementary and secondary schools.

This control over education has grown with little or no planning. Receipt of aid from the state was accompanied by the need for making reports. Gradually, this led to compliance with other state requirements. Personnel were needed to check and to file, and structure and policy became complex. More persons were needed to decide which districts would get how much and when. "Inspection" as law enforcement became the core of the thinking of some state department personnel.

Obviously, such lack of vision is not good enough today. There should be order for such a duty, not chaos. Legal provisions pertaining to state boards need overhauling. Surely, there should be a nonpartisan, lay, state board of education in each of the 50 states. This board should be composed of a group of citizens who represent the general public and who are elected. The powers and duties of the chief state school officer would be outlined in the law, briefly but clearly. It is he who is appointed by the elected board.

Local Organization for Public Education

Most state legislatures have delegated administrative authority to organize and to operate schools to local school districts. All school boards are subject to the state and its laws. They are established to enforce state laws relating to public schools.

A unified area of legal control over education may be termed many things: an administrative area, administrative unit, or a school district. There were about 35,000 of them at the start of the decade of the 1960's, and they represented numerous plans of organization. In the South, the political county is the unit of local school administration. In some large cities, there may be more than one school district. A high school district may be superimposed on a common school district, each with its separate board of education. Elementary and high schools are often operated by a single board.

Whatever the label, the piece of territory designated to operate public schools is not a sovereign power. A subordinate government, it is a mere taxing area. The school district is sometimes referred to in the press as "a department of local government." Not so! A school district, whatever its boundaries, is a separate and distinct unit from a city or town, even though fiscally dependent upon it. Cities, towns, and boroughs are governed by their own codes. Schools act under a state school code. Amendment of local laws does not by implication amend or repeal provisions of the school code.

Even though school government of a city is distinct from that city's civil government, school districts are usually subject to the police power of the municipality. Boards of education must operate the schools with regard to building and health regulations. Any higher governmental authority may take the real property of a lower governmental authority.

In some school districts, the school board delegates executive activity as a complete unit to the superintendent as its chief executive officer. The superintendent then is held fully responsible for the successful execution of board policies. In large systems there may be assistant superintendents. The assistant may be assigned to so many schools within the district or he may be head of an activity. Each operates solely under authority delegated from the chief executive and, for purposes of school administration, is under the control of the executive. In this type of organization, the superintendent has charge of instruction. He is responsible solely for relations with the board. He recommends financial policies and seeks to interpret those policies to the public. Research and curriculum occupy his immediate attention. He leaves the noninstructional activities to experts in child accounting, personnel records, supplies, plant, and finance. In this plan, instruction is dominant; specialized activities are subordinated.

In a second plan of organization, instruction may be headed by one person and business activities headed by another. Each reports directly to the board regarding his own province. The board acts through standing committees. Instruction does not dominate here.

In still another arrangement, the board of education may delegate executive activity to more than two coordinate divisions. The executive function is divided into several executive committees: those of instruction, business, finance, buildings, and auditing. Each committee functions coordinately but independently. Here, instruction is merely one of five areas of board interest. In this plan executive activity may be shared between the superintendent, secretary, and architect. Each reports to a special committee of the board. The school board acts as the coordinator.

In any plan, regardless of label, the superintendent is the agent of the board. Technically, it is the board that administers. No fundamental difference exists between the simplest organization under the smallest district system and the most complex. Authority may be delegated to one person by the board. The board must give its official approval to the acts of that person. The school board formulates policy which empowers, informs, and guides. Some bases for action can be extrastatutory, with duties and responsibilities outside specific law. A superintendent must deal with supervisors of special subjects, atypical children, and preschool children. He must help decide the scope of duties of such personnel as physicians, dentists, nurses, psychologists, and librarians. He must be concerned with duties and responsibilities of custodians, engineers, gardeners, secretary-clerks, and cafeteria managers.

School boards have been slow to share power with their chief administrative officers. Unfortunately, some school executives have not been particularly zealous in pursuing educational excellence. A competent administrator has to be concerned with problems of organization and with articulation of units within the over-all structure, so that continuity exists from the kindergarten through the twelfth or fourteenth grade. He must give attention to organizing people, positions, and things. He can organize efforts by recognizing such factors as time and space limitations. The school principal must see to it that the building in his care works as a unit. There are parents, teachers, clerks, custodians, and central office personnel to concern him.

Whatever the plan, the principal knows that the educational edifice is really "organization within organization." If there are advisory councils, to whom do they report? For what reasons? What is the organization of the central office staff so as to provide for needed services? Besides the formal organization, established by law and custom and declared into being by chart and outline of duties, how best can the principal deal with informal organization— person-to-person relationships built on casual and unofficial lines of communication?

Local organization is beset with many problems. Some are of a legal nature and some are not. Courts are called upon to adjudicate disputes of the former nature. Discretionary powers of school officials have been challenged most frequently. In the absence of a statute clearly granting authority to a school district—say, for organizing school classes for trainable children—the power to act may be challenged in the courts. As long as a school board acts in good faith, in the interest of the public, and does not violate statutes, courts are reluctant to interfere with discretion. They move slowly to declare a board regulation unreasonable, not substituting their discretion for that of school authorities.

Courts will interfere with acts of a school corporation if it abuses discretion or acts in bad faith. Because there is the presumption of validity regarding the acts of a school district (board of education), the one who challenges the exercise of discretion has the burden at law of proving its abuse. The duties called ministerial —as opposed to those that are judicial or discretionary—may be compelled to be performed by a citizen through the legal writ of mandamus. Quasi-judicial functions and discretionary acts are not subject to mandamus except to the extent of compelling a school board to make decisions regarding such matters.

CHAPTER IV

Pupils, Employees, and School Law

Law Affecting the Pupil

Admission.   From the day that a parent seeks admission for his child to the public school (maintained at state expense), the child is confronted with legal prescriptions. Regardless of pressures from the home, the child will not be admitted to the school unless he meets the requirements of age, health, residence, intelligence, vaccination, and cleanliness. The birth certificate must be available. His health is a matter of school concern, as are his mental abilities, residence, and (in some instances) his race and color. As he advances in school, he will be checked for scholarship. For his parents, transportation and payment of fees will raise legal questions.

However, the fact that the child may not immediately meet the conditions imposed for admission does not give school authorities any cause to refuse him admission outright. The courts have ruled that, if at all possible, school authorities must try to qualify the child for admission. Opinion is that "the statutory obligation to cause children to attend school involves an obligation to put them into condition to attend, and cannot be escaped by neglect to qualify them for attendance."

In an early case,[1] parents sought to compel admission of their children without the required physical examination. The Supreme Court of the state reiterated the principle that health regulations lie within the police power of government. Those who wish to enjoy the benefits of the public school must submit to conditions imposed by the state. As a result, government may legally prevent the admission to schools of individuals who might endanger the health, safety, and morals of themselves and other minors.

Residence is closely tied to admission. For school purposes, the term is not restricted to the parents' domicile. It refers to the actual residence of the child himself. Ordinarily, a child's legal residence is where his father lives. If his parents are legally separated and the

---

[1] *Streich* v. *Board of Education*, 34 S.D. 169, 147 N.W. 779 (South Dakota, 1914). For other information on school admission, see 47 Am. Jur. "Schools" secs. 147, 151–159, 191–199, and 216–219.

boy lives with his mother, her residence is his for school purposes.

Courts have permitted free admission to local public schools of the district where the homes are located. Upon a parent's request, a court may compel action to admit a child to a school. The court, however, will not compel school authorities to accept without fee a nonresident pupil. This lies entirely within the discretion of the board. If school officials feel that a hardship is imposed upon some by such a policy, application for relief must be directed to the legislature. Courts have no power to settle such matters.

Once having gained admission, the pupil has no legal right to insist that he be admitted to one particular class or to one certain group. A local school board need not make room for every child who applies to a particular school. Such placement is the prerogative of the district, if and when the basis for classification is reasonable. If the child is refused enrollment in a particular class, the parent may appeal to the proper administrative authorities, but he must exhaust such remedies before seeking aid of the courts.

The privilege of receiving an education at state expense may be refused to any person or class of individuals as the state orders. The "right" of the parent to have his child admitted to the public school to receive "free" schooling is civil rather than private. This means that education is a "political privilege" held in common with other qualified persons. There is no private right to be educated, resting upon authority within the federal Constitution.[2] Growing out of state citizenship, admission to a state's public school system is an immunity belonging to the person because he is a citizen of the state wherein he resides.

Even though a parent objects to a room and teacher assignment for his child, he must accept such placement. Alternatives are to change attendance areas, pay costs of nonpublic instruction, or furnish equivalent home tutoring. In other words, the home of the pupil may be considered as a "private school," providing the instruction given is "of the type contemplated by law."

No school board can force a married minor to remain in school if he chooses not to attend, the theory being that marriage emancipates the minor from parental authority. Courts here state that a school board may not refuse a child of school age, and who is married, the right or privilege of attending school. The reasoning for admitting a married minor rests upon the notion that it is com-

---

2 *Flory* v. *Smith,* 145 Va. 164, 134 S.E. 360 (Virginia, 1926).

mendable for a married person of school age to want to further his education.

In addition to requirements for getting into a public school, the pupil comes into direct contact with the law on other scores. Remaining parts of this section deal with compulsory attendance once the child is admitted; with the scope of school discipline; with some examples of reasonable school conduct rules; with legal restrictions regarding the curriculum; with the purchase of insurance to guard against costly injuries; with transportation to school; with the levying of fees; with the availability of the pupil's academic and personal records; and with regulations that may be imposed on participation in out-of-class activities.

School attendance.   When parents just discuss school, questions about attendance arise. Besides the age when a child may legally enter, parents wonder about the requirement that a child must attend each school day. In other words, why cannot a mother take the child on a shopping trip? Why does the principal's office bother to telephone the home the day the child is absent? Why does a report of absence send the attendance officer to the home? Why should the visiting teacher check on home-school relations? Does she have any right to pry? Both parent and child may wonder how many years a youngster must attend school before he can quit. Some question the need for a minor to get a permit to work and the right of the state to force a 15-year-old to go to continuation school if he drops out of regular school.

Such regulations concerning school attendance are not always understood by school personnel, and parents and pupils rarely understand them. The teacher must be informed about them. He is the one important link—the liaison between many homes and one school. The principal should aid the teacher to see fully the bases for school attendance regulations.

More than half of the 50 states require children between certain ages to attend school. Penalties for violations are imposed upon the parents of children who do not attend as required by law. When attendance officers seek the aid of a court in enforcement of compulsory attendance laws, they may seek a judgment which takes the form of a fine or imprisonment of the parents. School authorities may attempt to have the child committed to a home on the theory that he is being neglected. The state cannot depend solely upon the willingness of the parent to send his child, upon the complaints of neighbors, or upon actions of local police. Laws requiring attendance of children at school are not self-enforceable.

The attendance by law of almost every child means being confronted by an individual called "teacher." School personnel, with the teacher at the very center of the picture, have the task of providing the environment in which the child can and wishes to perform required tasks. It is the teacher who helps enforce the state compulsory school laws when he sends his daily report of violators to the school office. In acute cases, the teacher has the duty to notify the parent (or guardian of the child) in writing of the truancy, and that the case is being reported through the principal's office to the attendance officer.

Parents have the legal right to send their children to a nonpublic school if they prefer. The compulsory school law is complied with in so doing, since government does not compel school-age children to attend or meet the legal hurdle by getting private instruction. A case cited as an example of the right of parents to send children to a nonpublic school is one from Oregon.[3]

Prior to the enactment of new school codes in some states, compulsory attendance laws permitted a child to leave school when he had completed the course provided in his own school district. Age, not the attainment of a specified level of instruction, is now the crucial factor. In school districts where no high schools had existed, no compulsion existed for children to attend school beyond the eighth grade. Even with the new codes, in some states children who live great distances from schools are excused from attendance unless transportation facilities are available.

Since World War II, some states have authorized early childhood education as part of a complete public school program. Nursery school and kindergarten, although part of public education in larger districts, are not included in compulsory school laws. The war encouraged other changes in traditional school age limits. Exceptions have been made by legislation providing for the education of veterans. States which have constitutional free-school age limits may provide for free attendance beyond such limits. The principle is that these limits merely stipulate the minimum required.

Range of school discipline. A board of education inherently possesses the authority to make rules for management of schools. Except for clear signs of a contrary intent by the legislature, a

---

[3] *Pierce* v. *Society of Sisters,* 268 U.S. 510 (Oregon, 1925). Sisters operated a parochial school and sought to restrain enforcement of the Oregon compulsory school law which required all children to attend public schools.

board of education may repose in members of the professional teaching staff, including the superintendent, authority to establish rules controlling pupil conduct. Through custom, control is the task of the teachers and principal in each building. When the board fails to provide details for conduct, teachers, principal, and superintendent may make and enforce reasonable rules to maintain the efficiency of the school.

The school principal—along with some teachers and pupils chosen to participate in school government—decide on what are the pressing conduct problems. The principal must know the "house rules" established by teachers. None may run counter to school regulations and to policies of the board of education. Profanity, fighting, rudeness, slovenliness, bullying and similiar forms of behavior are usually interpreted by the teacher and are not described in board policy.

On the other hand, the principal must take direct charge of some types of misconduct. It is he who directly rules out alcoholic beverages in school, at school events, and en route between home and school. It is he who acts directly against the use of drugs. For health and safety reasons, he should see that smoking is discouraged. He must restrict the places where petting could occur.

School discipline includes suspension and expulsion. Who may do what and on what grounds? A school board is authorized to expel a pupil for violating board regulations. It possesses the legal power to take from the pupil for a time, the privilege of continuing his free public education in the school district. For expulsion, the pupil must have violated a reasonable rule or regulation. A principal may not expel. Such decision may be made only by the board. It is well established that a teacher may "go to the office" to request suspension of a pupil for his having committed an offense impairing orderly pursuit of instruction. Or, circumstances could arise where the welfare of a class might depend upon action taken by the teacher without recourse to the principal. The teacher might remove the pupil in question from all school activities and segregate him from his fellow classmates. This, however, is temporary action only.

Discipline in the school is broad enough to allow use of physical force in instances where the law states such use clearly or where the law is silent. Provision for corporal punishment (for any pupil who violates a proper rule) is within the broad authority reposed in the school board. Such punishment is usually not required but may be chosen by a teacher (with knowledge of the principal) for the child who disobeys a proper order.

Corporal punishment is allowed in many states and school districts for any improper conduct of a pupil. State laws dealing with punishment are of several types. The majority of states do not prohibit the use of corporal punishment in the schools. Maryland law advocates, "Pour it on." Pennsylvania's admonishes, "Take it easy." This means a "qualified yes," using no brutality, with no blows on the head at all. In the District of Columbia and New Jersey, corporal punishment is prohibited by law. By board regulation, many local school districts prohibit any use of corporal punishment.

Even though a board does not provide for corporal punishment, under proper circumstances a teacher or principal has the right to administer such punishment. This means that the aim must be change in behavior and not humiliation before others. A teacher legally may inflict corporal punishment that is reasonable in degree, since the local school has the same right as a parent to use corporal punishment. A teacher's right is restricted, however, by the limits of his jurisdiction and responsibility. Suitable physical means of reaching the child are legal when he persists in misconduct. The teacher stands in place of the parent—in the legal position called *in loco parentis*.

Proper discipline means that punishment must be reasonable, not excessive, and not administered with malice. For the sake of mental health, corporal punishment should be administered in the presence of the principal. This procedure may avoid legal trouble. Perhaps the teacher should go even further and secure the consent of the parent or guardian of the child. Obviously, such tacit permission should be sought before the occasion.

Courts get those cases where degree of "reasonableness" is the issue. What constitutes moderate and sensible discipline is a question of fact. The jury decides this, not the court.[4] The court has the task of determining whether rules are reasonable. It has no authority, however, to review the findings of a school board with respect to the facts. The power to determine what constitutes disobedience lies within the board. A court does not substitute its

---

[4] The Iowa Supreme Court readily agreed in *Tinkham* v. *Kole,* 110 N.E. (2d) 258 (1961), that proper discipline was of vital importance. The court stressed, however, that reasonableness of the punishment was a matter of fact for the jury. Whether a teacher is liable for honest errors in judgment is a question of law, pertaining to the status of qualified privilege.

judgment for that of school authorities. The only exception is where fraud, corruption, oppression, or gross negligence is revealed. Excepting these, all questions are factual ones to be decided by a jury in a civil suit.

Civil and criminal liability are substantially different. Assault and battery is the use of force or violence upon or toward another person. When committed under certain instances, force is not considered assault and battery. This usually includes the lawful exercise of authority to restrain a pupil. The teacher may use physical force to protect himself from a pupil whom he is attempting to discipline. Even death of a pupil resulting from corporal punishment may legally be excused if the teacher's conduct was within the limits set forth in the statutes defining homicide. The teacher may be free from criminal suit for administering corporal punishment of a moderate character when necessary and where no law exists to the contrary.

Whenever a child gets involved in a legal battle, charges may be preferred by the parent. The child soon becomes the third party in the case. Both school and home come out better when persons realize that the law is a last resort. It deals only with "legal minima," not with what should be done. Teacher and parent might well devote thought to the policies and techniques that might be used in handling certain kinds of behavior problems. This lies beyond the competence of courts and juries. The law provides no answer as to when and at what point the pupil's parents should be called in to look at behavior problems. It sheds no light on changes that might be made in the scope of activities planned by the board so as to reach pupils who have behavior problems.

Examples of reasonable rules. A school principal is vested with authority to make reasonable rules and provide direction for pupil behavior. To aid him in such responsibility, the public school provides guides for reasonable conduct against which to test his behavior. A requirement that pupils perform specified school assignments at home is such a one. To a limited degree the regulation of pupil dress may be ventured by a principal without board approval. There must be a proper and visible purpose, however.

Other reasonable rules include forbidding pupils to leave the school grounds during school hours. The so-called "closed campus" rule is valid, with schools requiring pupils to remain on the grounds during recess and free periods so as not to patronize certain businesses near the school. Other valid regulations would include not wearing metal heel plates and a requirement that commencement exercises be attended in prescribed garb.

The school may enforce rules providing for detention of pupils after school hours. For disciplinary purposes, a teacher may detain a pupil for a reasonable time, depending upon the age of the child. With the advent of transportation by bus, the practice falls into the questionable category. If injury should occur while a normally transported—and thus protected—pupil is walking home, the teacher might be liable for any consequent injury. The insurance policy on the bus would not cover the child while walking home.

Assignment of pupils to particular grades or classes is a matter solely for school personnel. The school board has a duty of formulating policies for its schools. Rules regarding promotion of pupils into next classes, grades, or subject levels are valid when reasonable and enforceable.

School rules follow pupils when they leave school premises. School authority does not end entirely when the school day is over and pupils have left the school building and school grounds. Authority of the principal and school staff must extend into the twilight zone between school and home. The rule is well established that school authorities may govern the conduct of pupils while off the school grounds and outside of school hours. This extends even to the summer vacation weeks. Yes, school authority includes enforcement of all reasonable rules and requirements anywhere and at any time. If a pupil's conduct places a teacher and school in disrepute, the principal may bar that pupil's readmission to the school when it reopens. The rule is that a board of education may discipline a pupil for any act, no matter where or when committed, provided the act tends immediately and directly to destroy the discipline and impair the efficiency of the school.[5]

If state codes do not forbid students to belong to fraternities, local rules may forbid membership by public school students in so-called Greek letter groups. The rules may provide for punishment for violation by expulsion, or they may declare violators ineligible to participate in certain nonclass school activities. Even though meetings of pupils are held outside of school hours and in private homes with the knowledge and consent of the parents, the school board may outlaw such organizations. The basis is that the

---

[5] See Edwards, *The Courts and the Public Schools*, p. 610.

spirit encouraged within closed corporations militates against the general welfare of public schools.

Courts will interfere to prevent the enforcement of rules if authority to act has been exceeded. A rule has been declared unreasonable which deprives the child of school privileges except as a punishment for a breach of discipline or an offense against good morals. A pupil may be expelled for willful and malicious acts. A board, however, has gone too far when it requires a pupil to pay for a window pane that he negligently broke. The rule is an unreasonable one. The courts interfere when school rules deprive a pupil of rights to which the law entitles him, or which tend to alienate the pupil from parental authority, or which manifestly reach beyond the instructional sphere.

When a board fails to act, a writ of mandamus will serve to compel school authorities to perform a required act. Where an attempt is made to enforce an unreasonable rule, such enforcement may be restrained by an injunction. Pupils who are arbitrarily or maliciously treated because of board rules have a right of action for damages against school board members personally. In such cases the board member may not seek judicial protection behind the cloak of board immunity from suit.

Curriculum prescriptions.   Some students of school law believe that many of the issues about curriculum—even mandatory state law—are raised because "patrons, school boards, and school personnel do not know the law."[6] Many cases exist about such topics as the "American Heritage," "Bible Reading," "Anti-evolution laws," "Flag Salute," and "Narcotics Education."

The fundamental power to select the system of instruction and courses of study to be pursued in the public schools rests with the legislature. It is the state which possesses authority to require pupils to pursue particular studies. It can command pupils to take up studies essential to good citizenship. The mandate of the legislature over the curriculum is final and binding on all agencies and persons.

The state's power over curriculum has two main components: that exercised by the state legislature and its agencies, and that exercised by local boards. A course prescribed as one to be taught cannot, of course, be discontinued by local board action. Sometimes the state must concede to the prohibitions placed on its cur-

---

[6] One is Madaline Kinter Remmlein who states the idea in "Statutory Problems," *Law and Contemporary Problems,* XX (Winter, 1955), 134.

riculum by actions of a federal court. So it was that a decision of the United States Supreme Court invalidated a statutory prohibition against teaching a foreign language in grades lower than the ninth.[7]

Whatever agency is given authority to select textbooks, action of the agency so designated is conclusive. The pupil and his parent have no voice whatever in this curricular matter. Some statutes expressly provide that the school committee of each town (or that each board) shall select the books for use in schools under its control.

Participation by pupils in a ceremony such as giving allegiance to the flag by saluting it is one curricular issue. The school has no power to make or enforce any requirement which the board cannot legally impose.[8] Such regulations are not legitimate conditions to school attendance, and therefore are illegal curricular activities. What can be required and what should be made optional, however, depends upon value judgments. The courts are involved here too. Parents may feel that the school supports religious activities when a Bible is read as part of the program. Actual instruction in religious dogma is prohibited by all states. Perhaps not enough attempts are made in public schools to limit and control the many sectarian influences found there.

Protection through insurance. Insurance coverage for pupils— to guard against costs involved in damage suits—is a protection of fairly recent origin. Quite naturally, parents want children protected from harm while at school. The purchase of coverage is one method of sharing high costs involved in injury. The chance of serious accidents at school-connected activities is considerable. There may be injury to pupils in and about the school building; while on field trips; related to the safety patrol program and school transportation in general; to other persons resulting from activities of pupils or employees; and at athletic contests and other out-of-class activities.

It should be understood that there is generally no liability on the part of a school district for injury to pupils, even though the state orders pupils to be in school. In most states parents cannot place the financial burden on government in case of serious injury to children while under school supervision. The plain fact is that there is no liability in most districts for failure to repair defective

---

[7] *Meyer* v. *Nebraska,* 262 U.S. 390, 43 S. Ct. 625 (1923).

[8] *West Virginia State Board of Education* v. *Barnette,* 319 U.S. 624, 147 A.L.R. 674 (West Virginia, 1943).

appliances, or for dangerous conditions of school grounds. Even though the doctrine of governmental immunity is supported by hundreds of school cases,[9] the trend now is to hold school districts liable for some negligent acts.

The purchase of insurance for protection against costs of injury is demanded due to the trend toward modification of the non-liability doctrine. Courts are starting to point in the direction of less injustice, but as yet they have not interpreted laws in such a way as to give judicial aid to injured pupils. Such laws are "strictly construed" since they abrogate the long-standing common law. California has gone further than any other state in altering the old law and making government financially responsible for costs of injury to pupils. The state allows direct suit against the school board, requiring that it, in case of school fault, pay damages out of school funds.

A board may pay out funds for premiums and not purchase protection for pupils. Purchase of insurance does not guarantee protection for an injured pupil if the policy protects only the district. Unfortunately, the average parent knows only that "there is insurance somewhere." Unless the policy contemplated so states *in writing* (or unless state law gives the right), a pupil injured at some school activity by an employee of the insured may not recover from the insured's (district's) insurance company.

Details of policies must be read. Some cover transportation injuries only, while others cover all types. A school board may include athletes in its coverage. The board may still cling to its "cloak of governmental immunity." Automobile insurance owned by a teacher or the district may not cover accidents when the mishap is not connected with any car owned by either the teacher or the district. If insurance cannot be legally written to protect the district, the bus driver himself should carry a liability policy. It can then be deposited with the district. If not, a parent may not be able to recover from a negligent driver who is unable to pay judgments. Insurance may be taken out by pupils to cover accidents. If taken by all—or nearly all—pupils, coverage is available at low group rates. This type of insurance markedly reduces the possibility of costly litigation, since an injured person is more nearly sure of financial relief.

School boards carry liability insurance so that tax moneys are

---

9 Remmlein, *School Law,* p. 280.

not used to pay damages. When judgment is obtained against a defendant district, money damages are paid by the insurance company. School district money is tax revenue collected for educational purposes only, not to pay damages.[10]

For the district to use money to buy insurance coverage, the immunity rule must be altered. When it is, problems are raised which cannot be dodged. One of most concern is: Should a school board carry coverage in order to have insurance funds available for payment of damages to injured pupils? The courts say that a statute authorizing the purchase of insurance by a district does not abrogate the common-law rule of governmental immunity of the school board, when acting within its governmental sphere.

Most courts have stated that without legislation permitting government to purchase accident insurance, a school board has no authority to do so under its general power to operate schools. Having no liability, the board has nothing to insure. Even with an enabling law, courts say that legislation permitting a board to buy protection for pupils does not mean that a suit may be taken against the board to establish the amount of damages for the insurance company to pay.[11] In pupil-injury cases, a court may find a school board not liable, the principal not liable, but the teacher guilty of negligence. In reference to school insurance:

> Probably nowhere in the entire body of school law is there more uncertainty, more realization of the gap between the moral and the legal duty of the school board—between the social and the legal rights of the public-school pupil.[12]

The law is slowly moving in the direction of protecting injured pupils by giving them access to insurance or to school district funds. The immunity rule is being changed outright by lawmakers or crumbled by the exceptions made constantly by courts. Parents can see to it that state law permits or requires boards of education to carry liability insurance. It is sound policy that school districts should be required by law to pay for damages for injuries. With this should come a planned program for accident prevention to avert costly court action.

---

[10] Madaline Kinter Remmlein, "Tort Liability of School Districts, Boards, and Employees," in *Law and the School Business Manager,* ed. Lee O. Garber (Danville, Ill.: Interstate Printers and Publishers, Inc., 1957), Chap. VIII, p. 195.

[11] Remmlein, *School Law,* p. 280. Even a "safe-place" statute imposes no board liability where improper construction causes a pupil injury.

[12] *Ibid.,* p. 281.

School transportation.   There is a relation between school transportation and insurance. The reason for separating the content is that other issues besides injury and liability are rightly included under the topic of "school transportation."

Perhaps the greatest proportion of school accidents occurs because of bus transportation in some 30,000 school districts within the 50 states. This is not at all surprising when one pupil out of five is transported daily—for some 180 round trips—by means provided by boards. In some districts more than half of the pupils are transported.

Parents, teachers, and members of boards of education should realize that "school transportation" may not be construed to include all activities just because pupils are involved. Statutes uniformly permit the transportation of pupils to and from school. Most of these laws do not, however, authorize the use of school-owned transportation to get pupil-participants or spectators to school-sponsored events. Such practices are then outside the law.

In order to have the largest possible measure of protection for transported pupils, the board should have in its minutes a definition of curriculum that is broad enough to include nonclass activities away from the campus. Where state laws prohibit such interpretation, pressure should be exerted on the legislature to get such activities within the law. Where a twilight zone exists, a prudent board encourages the pupil, teacher, and bus driver to carry the insurance which will help defray the costs of possible litigation and damages.

Some state transportation laws permit suit to be brought to the extent of bus insurance. The defense of governmental immunity must not then be raised. At one time it was thought that denying the defense of governmental immunity solved the problem. Minnesota was one of the first states to require an endorsement on all school-bus insurance policies indicating such a waiver. The courts stated that governmental immunity could not be so waived.

Another problem in transporting pupils is keeping within the legal limit regarding numbers of pupils that may be taken in a single bus load. No legal precedent exists for a schoolbus driver to wait for a pupil who has been kept in school because of disciplinary measures.

The United States Supreme Court upheld legislation which provided for the reimbursement from tax funds to parents for payment of bus fares for parochial school children.[13] This was considered desirable since the children could then ride buses to and from schools rather than run the risk of hazards incident to walking or "hitch-hiking."

School costs. The "free" public school is not without charges. School attendance "at no cost" means that no tuition is charged pupils who are within certain ages and who reside within the school district. In other words, public schooling is free to children who can profit from education and who are at least six years old and below 21. A public school district may not charge tuition for bona fide residents who meet requirements. Incidental fees may be charged, however, without violating the requirement of free schooling.

The school principal is customarily responsible for all student fees collected. He must make a regular report to the superintendent's office. These fees can be sizable. Although the "free" public school is heralded in the United States and abroad, close examination will disclose that even elementary school pupils must bring money for services conducted by the school but not supported by tax dollars. In the secondary school, charges for textbooks and for school-connected activities can run to "tuition-size" amounts.

Under state constitutional and statutory provisions, the schools are free for those children qualified for admission. Tuition may be charged nonresidents or pupils who are beyond the legal age limit. A school district may not charge tuition for residents. Fees are paid so that children may attend a school outside their resident district or so that they may attend a nonpublic school. It is usually the school district that arranges for its children to attend a school across a district boundary. This action may be due to the fact that grades nine through twelve are not provided, or that the district operates no schools at all, merely levying taxes for school purposes. These tuition charges are paid out of public school funds of the resident district. When a parent arranges for his own children to attend a school outside his district, it is the parent who pays tuition costs.

Fee-paying provides the basis for considerable court action. In Iowa, a court stated that children were entitled to free schooling without the county having to pay tuition to the district in which the pupils attended school. The issue was one of "legal indigency."

---

[13] *Everson* v. *Board of Education,* 330 U.S. 1 (New Jersey, 1947).

Through court action, a school district was able to prevent the children from actual attendance until the recalcitrant parent handed over the tuition to the receiving district.

The law and pupil records. Perhaps no group of workers exchanges more information about people than do those employed by schools. Both teacher and administrator comment about a pupil to other persons—teacher, administrator, parent, and prospective employer. Thus, it is usual for a teacher to have possession of information about pupils in the school.

Sometimes a school employee takes occasion to make unfavorable statements relating to the record of a pupil under his supervision. He may do this when asked to comment about conduct, reasons for school dismissal, or job recommendations. Making remarks about individual pupils in conversation and in writing is part of the educator's work. Making comments of a defamatory nature is not part of it. Information about academic records or behavior may be damaging.

Answers to questions about liability for defamation require taking a look at the term "privileged communication" and the word "defamation." Looking at defamation first, this is the commission of an intentional "tort" or legal wrong. It is not injury caused by pure accident or by carelessness. A defamatory statement is one communicated to a third person which tends to diminish the esteem and confidence in which the abused person is held. It excites adverse feelings or opinions against that person in the minds of a substantial and respectable minority of society.[14] Defamation describes the invasion of another's interest in his good name by the utterer's communicating words which tend to lower that person in the estimation of the community. The "publication" of the defamatory remarks involves any telling to a third person and holding the person up to disgrace or scornful insolence. When one does this orally, his conduct is called slander. When one is defamed by means of the printed word, the charge is one of libel.

The danger of being liable for uttering defamatory words is low. Usually, the employee speaks or writes within the protection of "privilege." If uttered with good intent by an employee to a legitimate hearer, the comment is protected by the theory of "qualified

---

14 Reynolds C. Seitz, "Law of Privileged Communications," in *Law and the School Principal,* ed. Seitz (Cincinnati, Ohio: W. H. Anderson Company, 1961), p. 153.

privilege." This protection is afforded so that the purposes of the school can be better realized. The transmittal of defamatory material is sometimes necessary. No injury can be claimed if the communication is made directly to persons whom the educator reasonably feels is qualified to use the material. When defamatory information is volunteered, a teacher may exceed his privilege. The law does not protect the communication of rumor and suspicion under nonprivileged conditions.

Surely the reason for such protection is clear. If not thus protected by law, employees might suppress truthful but embarrassing kinds of information. Truth would be buried through fear of law suits. One uttering unfavorable remarks could be spared only by accepting the heavy burden of proving the truth of his own remarks. The educator needs the assurance of privilege when he seeks to protect the interests of pupils, the school, and the public.

No blanket rule exists for knowing what facts and records of pupils may be released upon inquiry of prospective employers, school authorities, and institutions. However, in looking at comments made by educators in cumulative folders of pupils, the reader may find out something about the pupils represented therein. He is likely to discover a great deal more about the employee-writers. Facts and biases get interwoven—events with perceptions—so that impartial judgments about pupils are almost impossible to be drawn.

The educator owes a professional and moral responsibility to respect the rights of pupils. One of these is to separate what "he" did and said from what an adult believes to have happened. Honesty and integrity are served when the academic and personal records of pupils mirror actual occurrences plus sound personal judgments. If these contain defamatory data, privilege protects when shared with those who have a professional interest in the records. The "law of defamation" need not be an unwary trap for school people.

It is the duty of the local school to furnish honest and complete information about all competitors for academic awards. The judges of evidence as to the suitability of any one candidate for an academic award have no discretionary power.[15] They may not withhold information or distort information so as to influence the panel of judges. Pupils who meet eligibility requirements for entering competition for a scholarship have the vehicle of the writ of

---

[15] Madaline Kinter Remmlein, *The Law of Local Public School Administration* (New York: McGraw-Hill Book Company, 1952), p. 212.

mandamus to compel school authorities and the judges to act in good faith in recording and evaluating fitness for academic prizes.

A second matter pertaining to both defamation and privilege is that of releasing upon inquiry of local police unfavorable records pertaining to pupils. Without a court order, can such data be released with impunity to the F.B.I. or to other accredited governmental investigators? State laws and local regulations differ. Opinions of attorneys general have attempted to clarify the relationship which "ought to exist" between school people and the enforcement branch of government. Surely, information which will lead to detection of an offender can be communicated, provided that the law enforcement officer who asks for the information has the proper and valid authority to do so. This is based on the fact that everyone owes society the duty to assist in the discovery of crime, dishonesty, or other wrongdoing.

Nonclass activities program.   Teaching is no longer limited to instruction wholly within the classroom. Despite the marked change in the definition of "school curriculum" within the past generation, the supervision of such activities involves danger. A wise rule to follow is that no school employee, officer, or private association should supervise or conduct pupil activity programs contrary to authority exercised by the board of education. The excuse of "pupil interest or pressure" is simply not a valid legal defense if trouble occurs. This means all student activity—athletic and other out-of-class functions.

The superintendent has the duty to inform applicants of this fact. Before a teacher is employed by the board of education, the school superintendent should take the time to explain that teaching duties encompass both class and nonclass types of activity.

Law Affecting Teachers and Other Employees

Admittedly, some of the same law pertains to teachers and other employees as that stated under the previous section on "pupils and the law." Here, however, effort is made to indicate differences rather than similarities.

The differences are best noted by taking cognizance of the wide range of problems facing staff personnel and involving legal issues. These include: retirement, tenure, contracts, loyalty oaths, membership in organizations, employment status, academic freedom, the first teaching assignment, collective bargaining agents, leaves, professional growth, and the *in loco parentis* doctrine.[16]

Annuity or pension.   In all the states, public school employees are provided with some plan for retirement. The teacher must be a "permanent" employee to be covered; thus, allowances may be paid under specific provisions. The retirement plans are either state or local and are of the "gift" or "contract" type.

The real difference in plans hinges on the relationship between "who or what" contributes to the retirement fund. In other words, whether the teacher contributed to the retirement system is the single and most important factor in relation to any plan. Technically speaking (and in the retirement field it is a must to do so), a benefit financed by the employer only is called a "pension." An annuity is an annual allowance or income (may be paid out quarterly or monthly) which is the return from an investment of capital with accrued interest. Practically all retirement plans are "joint-contributory" plans in which both teacher and employer share a responsibility and from which fund the annuities are eventually paid.

The distinction is a crucial one. Courts hold that payment of a joint-contributory retirement allowance constitutes a contract. According to state and federal law, a contract may not be impaired. Chicago teachers challenged the constitutionality of an amendment to their retirement legislation which would reduce their "pensions."[17] Confusion arose because the statute originally setting up the plan had used the word "annuity" to describe what was actually a "pension." The allowances were not reduced. Looking at the nature of the arrangement rather than the label it bore, the court said the law had created vested rights.

Technical pension legislation may be changed by the legislature at any time, but outright gratuities may not be made from public funds to provide additional retirement dollars for which teachers perform no service. If additional benefits are wanted for retired teachers, the legislature must request that the involved teachers stand by for substitute service. For presently employed full-time teachers, most legislatures may authorize the levy of state taxes for additional retirement dollars. To this, teachers would add their own contributions.

---

[16] See Leo M. Chamberlain and Leslie W. Kindred, *The Teacher and School Organization* (Englewood Cliffs, N.J.: Prentice-Hall, Inc., 1958).

[17] *Dodge* v. *Board of Education of Chicago,* 302 U.S. 74 (1937).

Tenure laws. Controversy over tenure rights continued to occupy much of the energies of courts at the start of the 1960's. Teacher tenure legislation comes before the courts for interpretations of intent and scope of benefits.

The nature and purpose of tenure laws are far from being well understood by teachers and administrators. There are some who assume that tenure is a status attained by all teachers. On the contrary, many of the statutes regulating the duration of teachers' contracts are not statewide in application. In some states, teachers in certain school districts are not covered by tenure. Some teachers may be included in separate laws for different types of districts. States have more than 50 laws pertaining to contract length. Only about a third of these are statewide. All these laws prescribe continuing contracts or tenure employment for teachers. They apply to all, or nearly all, certificated employees.

Reasons for enactment of tenure laws are not obscure. Abuses which resulted in the enactment of the first civil service act provided the stimulus for such legislation. Another was the sound public policy of protection of the educational interests of the state. Tenure helps make the teaching corps more stable. It discourages boards of education from putting their prime concern on saving money by employing teachers who have built up no salary increments.

Tenure laws are sometimes called continuing-contract laws, civil service laws, or "fair dismissal" laws. Regardless of title, all such laws contain security features. Teachers, however, may have salary downgraded without violating rights. Under some tenure laws, teachers are afforded no protection whatsoever from such salary reductions, demotions, or arbitrary transfers within the school system.

The courts state that there is no demotion where no salary difference exists between the former position and the new position, and where no difference exists between the two positions in importance of duties, dignity accorded, responsibilities shouldered, authority wielded, or prestige attached thereto. One principle is clear: A teacher does not acquire tenure in any one particular position. For example, assignment of a junior high school teacher to a sixth grade is no demotion. If a reassignment is a real demotion, it is considered equivalent to discharge for unsatisfactory service. Except by prescribed procedures, this may not be accomplished legally by a board of education.

Tenure legislation is not based upon contractual relations between the state and affected teachers. Through tenure, teachers are protected in their positions from political interference and from arbitrary dismissal. Tenure does not, however, assure permanent jobs at public expense. Courts have been reluctant to restrict the power of subsequent legislatures, leaving tenure and contract separate unless the statutes clearly so intend. The theory is that sovereign power to enact laws to improve education cannot be bartered away by the legislature itself. The notion here is that the educational interests of the state are always paramount to private interests of teachers.

The common law recognizes authority of the local board to discharge a teacher for sufficient cause during a contract period, regardless of tenure status. Exactly what constitutes sufficient cause cannot be stated categorically.[18] Customary reasons for removal include the charge of inefficiency, insubordination, incompetency, refusal to answer questions, and failure to subscribe to oaths. Tenure teachers may be dismissed for such charges as "conduct unbecoming a teacher" and "unprofessional conduct." Presumably, such "reasons" are more specific than the vague charge in Colonial times of having an "adulterous look in one's eye." However, the blanket charges could embrace such specific acts as gambling, drinking intoxicants while on duty, fighting on or off school property, quarreling in public, being arrested, paying fines, getting excessive publicity, or exhibiting conduct unbecoming an American.

Teachers may be dismissed during their contract period for immorality even if there is no express statute permitting such dismissal. A tenure teacher may be legally discharged for discussion in his high school class of the price range of prostitutes.[19] When statutes list the causes for which a teacher's certificate may be revoked, it may not be revoked for other reasons than those so enumerated. The presumption is that any detailing of reasons in-

---

[18] Robert R. Hamilton and E. Edmund Reutter, Jr., *Legal Aspects of School Board Operation* (New York: Bureau of Publications, Teachers College, Columbia University, 1958), p. 64. The conditions under which a teacher can be removed from his position are governed by the provisions of his contract and by state law. All provisions of the constitution, state statutes, and pertinent prescriptions of state agencies are part of the contract—the mutual promise idea—along with local board rules.

[19] *State ex rel. Wasilewski* v. *Board of School Directors of the City of Milwaukee*, 111 N.W. (2d) 198 (1961).

cludes all grounds for revocation. Inability of a teacher to perform duties does not necessarily mean "incompetency." Any properly certified teacher has the presumption of competency on his side, and the burden of proving incompetency rests upon the board. If the board fails in that proof, the teacher may not legally be discharged, regardless of how thoroughly convinced the board may be of "incompetency."

Statutes emphasize the necessity for following prescribed procedures for teacher dismissal. These must be followed if discharge is contemplated at the close of the school year as well as during the year. A statement of reasons for dismissal must accompany notice of termination. Under some statutes the teacher receiving the notice must request the reasons himself. In holding a hearing, the board should confront the teacher with persons who made the charges. The accused is entitled to present evidence in his own defense. He may have counsel and have witnesses testify in his behalf.

When dismissal is contemplated during the term of a teacher's contract, certain procedural rights can be demanded as a requirement of "due process." This relates in no way to tenure rights. Discharge during the year is governed by contract law. Thus, provisions for a hearing prior to dismissal of a tenure teacher pertain to the constitutional guarantees of due process.

How permanent is tenure? "Not very" must be the answer. Boards may discharge teachers for adequate cause even if statutes are silent. Tenure employees, however, can be dismissed only for specific cause and then only in the manner prescribed by law. The distinction is real between failure of a board to renew a contract which has expired and discharge of a teacher during the contract period or under a tenure statute. Continuing-contract legislation differs from tenure legislation because a teacher employed under a continuing contract may be notified of nonreemployment at the end of the school year, regardless of cause and without having any reason stated.

Certificates, licenses, and contracts.   Courts are in agreement that a teacher must show evidence of preparation before taking up duties. Possession of a certificate or license is a prerequisite to obtaining a contract.

Despite use of the separate terms "certificate" and "license" in statutes and the literature, no valid reason exists for doing so. A certificate is a testimonial—a statement in writing certifying the

holder to have completed requirements for the particular occupation. A license is a legal permit, usually issued by a governing
body. A license (or certificate) is in the nature of a commission.
On what it considers valid grounds, a state board of examiners
may refuse to grant the petitioner a certificate (license) to teach.
A mere license is revocable, and there is no constitutional right
to be employed just because one has the necessary certificate. In
other words, a license granted by the state certifying agency does
not entitle the holder to demand a teaching position. The document merely shows that the holder may be legally employed in a
position for which he can qualify.

A certificate has none of the elements of a contract. It is not a
property right. Most state laws are unclear as to when a teaching
certificate must be acquired. They indicate that it must be valid
throughout the period of service. In contrast to the teaching contract, a license to teach is a mere privilege conferred by the state.
It is always held, subject to any laws in force at the time of issuance
or any future legislation providing for its forfeiture. New and additional burdens may be placed upon holders of certificates.

The legal significance of the certificate is that it is a license to
practice a profession. School boards are prohibited from employing noncertified persons. A teacher is legally qualified when he has
been certified. A certificate is *prima facie* evidence of competence.
A local board may, however, establish reasonable qualifications
for its own teachers beyond those required for minimum state certification. Many types of employment policies exist, depending
upon community wishes as evidenced in board procedures. No
statute is needed to make the use of eligibility lists legal.

Teaching contract. As one contracts, so is he bound. States
must not pass legislation impairing the obligation of contracts. These
two legal maxims are at the heart of contract law.

The law applicable to voluntary legal relationships has assumed
a position of increasing importance. In primitive society, the law
enforced only crude rights. Modern business would collapse without the "good faith" which contract law provides. The source of a
teacher's right to his job is not statutory but contractual. It is necessary to take a look at what a contract is and what it does. Records
show that the teacher "breaks" the agreement more often than the
board does. Some who call themselves members of a profession will
enter into agreements with several boards, waiting for the best
offer and not stopping to think what their actions imply.

No mystery surrounds a contract. It is an agreement in good faith which creates an obligation. Through "consideration" and "mutual consent," two or more parties come under obligation to the other. Each reciprocally acquires a right to whatever is promised by the other. The law recognizes the performance of the promise as a duty. Offer of a position and an acceptance is the core of the promise. The contract is the document; but, more important, it is the relationship evidenced by the piece of paper.

Since a contract rests upon a "promise," the concern in contract cases is whether an enforceable promise was made. Courts look to see if some expression of a common intention was made by at least two persons to establish legal obligations. A contract was entered into if (1) two or more persons were involved; (2) a definite common intention existed; (3) intention was actually communicated by one to the other; (4) intention referred to legal relationships; and (5) the terms in the agreement affected the parties personally.

Terms of a contract may be gathered from a number of sources. Statutory provisions are read into a teacher's contract, as well as rules and regulations of state and local boards. By implication, each becomes a part of the employment agreement.

A teaching contract is for specific performance of services. The question arises: If a teacher should decide that he does not want to teach, can he be forced to do so? From reported cases, a teacher has the legal duty to meet such obligations as the contract imposes. The teacher's failure or refusal without justification constitutes a breach of contract.

Public contracts depend on conformity with law. In order for a board to enter into a valid agreement, it must act as a unit. All members must have had notice of the meeting and an opportunity to attend. A school board may ratify any contract which it had authority to make. It may ratify an invalid contract but not a void one. When ratified, this contract is considered as valid in its entirety and from inception. A contract beyond the board's powers is unenforceable. The other party cannot collect damages because he is presumed to know the extent of the powers of a public body. The courts, however, look to substantial rather than literal performance of contracts.

Board officials are not personally liable for honest mistakes in judgment. There is, however, no remedy in the courts when school authorities exercise their legal powers unwisely. The courts will support a board's authority to rescind any action which it may have taken, however unwise, at any time before rights to third parties have vested. The courts will cancel out any contract in which it is shown that self-interest of a board member in a contract conflicts with the performance of official duty.

As legal instruments, oral contracts are as effective as written ones. When statutes require employment agreements to be written, contracts with teachers must be in writing.

Regardless of legal requirements, contracts for teaching should always be written. Such a procedure avoids possible misunderstandings. When a contract is reduced to writing, even the preliminary negotiations cannot be confused. What was decided upon is in the document. Signatures are signed to agreed upon terms. In this way, both teacher and district are protected. Oral statements then cannot contradict terms of the written instrument. It is usually held that there can be no recovery for the reasonable value of services rendered under an oral contract when the law requires a written one.

Cases are legion in which boards have become involved in legal controversies because of loose business practices in employing teachers. This fact should cause much concern to teachers and thoughtful board members. A teacher usually signs his contract without knowledge of the existence or nature of many board rules and regulations. It is wise for the board to check contracts against legal restrictions obtaining in the state and district. The board should pass a ratifying resolution on contracts of teachers in order that the record of such action appear in the minutes. The ethical teacher takes his contract seriously. He does not accept one position and then take another. Under no circumstances does he abandon a contract in the absence of a bona fide release. The honest teacher and serious board members can work together to strengthen the law and to force from the teaching profession those who would accept its privileges, but shun its obligations.

Obedience to oaths.   Laws requiring oath-taking by employees generally demand, as a condition to occupying a teaching position, that the employee subscribe to an oath attesting his loyalty to the government of the United States. Courts have sustained the right of school districts and educational institutions to require employees to so subscribe. The validity of a board rule requiring teachers to answer questions concerning their connections with the Communist Party was sustained in California.[20] The courts have sustained both a statute and board rule providing for dismissal of a teacher refusing to answer questions of lawful investigating committees concerning his connection with alleged subversive organizations.

One of the laws designed to ferret out disloyal teachers is the New York Feinberg law. Membership in subversive organizations there was made legal grounds for dismissal. The law states that Communists have infiltrated into the profession and are thus able to spread alien propaganda. The law requires an annual report on all school employees.

Constitutionality of the law was attacked on the basis that it violated the right of free speech. The majority of the United States Supreme Court said it did not.[21] One member of the court warned about "going too far" in protecting children at the expense of personal freedoms of teachers.

Academic freedom.   The idea of academic freedom is unfortunately thought of as referring mostly to college-level personnel. The schoolteacher can accustom himself to being part of the "go along with the crowd" philosophy. All teachers should act like self-respecting members of the profession. They should value difference and cherish opposing viewpoints. This value is stressed here in addition to the private rights of the teacher. Freedom of the teacher to become involved in community issues is both a matter of academic freedom and private right.

Undoubtedly, there are unwritten rules (mores and other social pressures) which circumscribe activities of public employees. Through the local pressures, the schoolhouse is used to promote the community's viewpoint (or at least that of the politically and economically sagacious) on social, political, economic, and religious issues. If one teacher chooses to champion an unpopular cause, all teachers may be subjected to harassment or censure.

The classroom teacher does not own the child's mind, but it is the teacher who must help the child see that whether a course of

---

[20] *Board of Education of City of Los Angeles* v. *Eisenberg,* 277 P. (2d) 943 (California, 1954). See 27 A.L.R. (2d) 487 for case material on rejection of teachers for disloyalty. Other cases of interest are: 342 U.S. 485; 163 A. (2d) 420; and 125 So. (2d) 554. Loyalty-oaths cases and those relating to removal of teachers for refusal to answer questions regarding Communist affiliations are related with different principles involved.

[21] *Adler* v. *Board of Education of the City of New York,* 342 U.S. 485, 72 S. Ct. 380 (1952).

action is right does not depend upon who in the community holds the idea. A courageous teacher must criticize local points of view, just as these are examined elsewhere. It is the teacher's responsibility to conduct fearless inquiry into relevant points of view concerning most controversial topics.[22] If he is dismissed for his contrariness, the professional group must back him. It must see that no qualified teacher applies for the vacancy. It should recommend that the school district have its accreditation suspended until school authorities there allow teachers to act as responsible adults.

What is academic freedom? It is the atmosphere created by the board and community leaders—an atmosphere which encourages teachers to act and practice their profession as adult leaders. It means getting the teacher down from his "ivory tower." It means that teachers abandon delegating strictly professional decisions to lay organizations in order "to get along better" with the spokesmen of the community.

If academic freedom were to be taken seriously by more teachers and by community leaders, then the belligerent attitude of teachers toward lay attackers, and of the attackers for the attacked, would gradually give way to one of mutual respect. The professional teacher would burden the courts with cases with the view to getting them to restrict the wide area of discretion of school boards so that personal rights and intellectual freedom of teachers could be made real.

Collective bargaining agreements.   With increased use of the tools of collective bargaining by employee groups in private industry since World War II, much attention has been paid to the problem of collective action by teacher groups. More and more interest is being centered around the right of teachers to organize into unions and thus bargain collectively.

The question is: To what extent can school boards legally agree to negotiate with teachers' organizations? The extent to which public employees and school board employees specifically can engage in collective bargaining had not, by the start of the 1960's, come to court tests in most states. A crucial element continues to be a matter of teacher strikes. Two large teacher groups have taken official positions against strikes. However, the word "strike" is not clear. To some, it means remaining away from the job "to get

---

22 Myron Lieberman, *Education As a Profession* (Englewood Cliffs, N.J.: Prentice-Hall, Inc., 1956), Chapter 3, "Authority in Education," pp. 49–86.

better conditions." To others, it means merely a weapon in the arsenal of employer-employee warfare.

It seems clear that public employers and employees cannot bargain collectively if the agreement contemplated includes either the right to strike against government or any closed shop provision. Different from private industry, collective bargaining cannot be practiced as "strategic weaponry" in public employment. A school board may not legally surrender authority and its prerogatives to employee organizations. In fact, some boards by law are without legal power to enter into collective bargaining with their personnel.

Regardless of what label is used, collective bargaining will continue to be a rallying point for the members of teacher groups. It represents much by way of personnel concerns for teachers. It affects the legal status of teacher unions and acceptance by the public of teacher unions. For some, the idea embodies the personal freedom to choose—to fight community prejudices and be master of the professional house of education.

Those who endorse the basic right of the teacher to affiliate with groups of his own choosing point to other professional workers who are unionized. They remind skeptics that several state courts have established a teacher's right to affiliate with a union. Whether a local board can refuse to employ union members is a matter of local policy. Unless specifically prohibited by such rule or statute, it seems clear that public employees—including teachers —can maintain membership in associations organized along occupational lines.

Absence from duty. The employee can enjoy "absence with official leave" if he plans ahead. State statutes usually set the minimums for teacher leaves of absence. Local rules can go beyond.

Granting of leaves may be made mandatory on local boards by state law. It may be discretionary in local districts. If statutes specify the bases and conditions of leaves for teachers, those are the only bases and conditions upon which leaves may be granted. A binding principle is that "a board of education cannot give away public money."

Leaves in the past have been provided mainly for sickness. Usually, the law states the number of such days with full pay available to the teacher. In addition, there are certain vacation days included in the annual contract. These can be labeled "leave days." It is customary for boards to grant teachers paid absences to attend professional meetings. Sometimes, teachers may visit other schools within the system or some distance away. As long as no extra compensation is involved, the teacher draws his regular salary for such activity.

Boards have arrangements for military leaves and those for professional improvement. These include study plans and travel. Unless the teacher is entitled to sabbatical pay, such leaves are granted with no sacrifice as to position. Salary cannot be paid ordinarily. A board may require a forced leave of a teacher, as in the case of pregnancy or mental incompetency.

Before any leave-taking, both teacher and board should come to agreement about status and benefits. If a leave occurred between the second and third year of a three-year contract, the nature and extent of a teacher's duties must be understood. Can he receive outside pay for work while under contract provisions? May the board legally raise his salary after his return, but during the period of the contract? Additional payments to a teacher under the original contract may be illegal, regardless of the source of funds. It is customary to recognize the legality of payments made to an employee under separate and independent agreements, whether on leave or not. If a board wishes to increase the salary of a teacher who is still under contract—and whom the board wishes to return because of his added skills—the board should terminate the original contract, with consent of the teacher. Then a new agreement can be entered into.

Courts usually support the teacher who sues to recover salary if and when a board forces a leave upon a teacher without cause. It is well settled that illegal authorization by the board of a leave of absence does not release the board from its obligations. As one contracts, so is he bound. A teacher can recover payment for the time when the board forced the leave.

Professional growth. Once a teacher has been awarded his certificate—his teaching credential—he may not choose to rest on previous laurels. Both the law and conscience prod him to further study. The law can specify "in-service" growth by making him do what he ought to do anyway. This might mean taking courses for credit (so that skills of reading, thinking, and writing are sharpened) or planned study and travel abroad.

The law can specify the provisions for the renewal of certification privileges. It can state how often teachers must reapply for certificates. But the law can go only so far. It is up to the teacher himself to build and then maintain professional communications. Few teachers show gross or flagrant incompetence. Some, however, become indifferent. This can give way to lack of interest to improve —both personally and professionally.

The responsibility for on-the-job instructional improvement rests squarely upon the building principal. Organized and conducted on the basis of plans approved by the superintendent, the in-service program officially begins in the principal's office. The law indicates that he is the "professional head of the school." He must be aware of the strengths and limitations of the teachers. If not, he falls far short of his legal duty as instructional leader. A recent case held that a school board may adopt a rule stating that a teacher be required to join a professional organization as a condition precedent to enjoying rights conferred by the salary schedule.[23] The case illustrates that a principal is on solid ground when he urges the board to make membership a requirement to advance on the salary schedule. Perhaps coercion by withholding pay is undesirable. It ought to be the task of the administrator to help all employees willingly to carry out the educational mandate of the state.

The principal is responsible for seeing that special laws pertaining to public education are observed. These include instruction that tells of the evils of the consumption of intoxicants and excessive use of tobacco and any use of narcotics without medical prescription. He has the duty to see that teachers observe national holidays and display placards in classrooms depicting the holidays. If viewed strictly, it would seem that schools in all 50 states perhaps break at least one school law every day.

The legal aspects of the relationship of employees to the principal are quite varied. There is confusion (not equaled elsewhere in the public school systems) about the principal's duties as required by law.[24] As head of the school, the principal comes into contact with many people. Some of the resulting problems have legal bases. He should recognize these so that he can help solve the problems rather than become a part of them. No teacher or layman can seriously expect the school principal to shoulder the whole load of instructional betterment. He is not a magician, or lawyer, or therapist. All, however, need to appreciate the legal requirements of his position.

---

[23] *Magenheim* v. *Board of Education*, 347 S.W. (2d) 409 (Missouri, 1961).
[24] Warren E. Gauerke, *Legal and Ethical Responsibilities of School Personnel*, p. 112.

CHAPTER V

School Officers and the Law

A public position may be a public office which represents public employment. A school board is composed of local officers. Courts classify elected persons as "officers" and appointed persons as "employees." The distinction is legally important in terms of duties and rights afforded each class.

Semantic Problems

The line between a public officer and an employee working for the public is "shadowy and difficult to trace." One of the problems arises over using terms that are not precisely defined. Some courts have held that a city school superintendent is a public officer.[1] Writers in school administration have stated that "the law recognizes the superintendent as a state official." If the chief executive of a school board is supposed to be *the* instructional leader, he had better be called an employee, not an officer. Also, an office held in the local school district is said by some to be a district office, not one of the state. The professional literature on school administration consistently classes the school superintendent as an employee of the local board. He stands in a purely contractual relation to a board. He cannot be regarded as being clothed with the privileges and prerogatives of public office. He performs his duties at the dictate of the board, whose members are officers. Teachers may refer to the "office of the superintendent," but they mean a place rather than a person who holds public office.

Authorities are not harmonious as to whether school personnel of the central "office" are public officers or local officers, or both state and public officers.[2] When the term "state officer" is used, it ordinarily excludes municipal or local officers. By law, school officers are state rather than municipal officers.

Regardless of label, what one is called should be governed by

---

[1] Newton Edwards, *The Courts and the Public Schools* (Chicago: University of Chicago Press, 1955), Chapter VI, p. 113 ff has cases cited showing some of the confusion.

[2] 78 C.J.S. 392, p. 827.

77

functions performed, not by methods of selection. The real question concerns the nature of service performed by the incumbent and of the duties imposed on him. Many of the characteristics of the position of public school teacher suggest that it could, in reality, be a public office. These are: The position is created by the legislature; it is concerned with public benefit; its powers and duties are fixed by law; the position rather than the person has permanency and continuity; it may require the taking of an oath; and the salary is fixed by law.

More important than what appears to be superficial similarities between the position of teacher and a public office is this fact: Some of the sovereign power of the state is delegated to an officer, never to an employee. Whatever part of governmental sovereignty is delegated in connection with public education, such part is delegated to the board, whose members are state officers. Wherever it appears that the duties are of an important character—involving the proper performance of some function of government—the person charged with them is properly regarded as a public officer.[3]

Certain terms are appropriate when a school officer, rather than a public employee, is being thought of. Reference is made to the eligibility and election and to the right to hold office after expiration of the official term. Consequences of failure to file the statutory bond refer only to officers. The status of officers may be *de facto* or *de jure*. There are incompatible offices, and there are modes of attack upon title to public offices.

In summary, there are at least four indispensable elements characterizing public office. The alleged office (1) must be created by the constitution, the legislature, or by a municipal body through authority conferred by the legislature; (2) must possess a portion of sovereign power used for public benefit; (3) must have powers conferred and duties to be discharged defined by the legislature or through its direct authority; and (4) must have permanency and continuity.[4]

Differences in requirements.   State laws require certain qualifications for school officers different from those pertaining to employees. The law often states that school officers must file a bond within a specified time after election or appointment. The law requires the officer to be chosen by popular vote. Special elections are

---

[3] 78 C.J.S. 948.
[4] Remmlein, *School Law* (2d ed.), pp. xxix-xxx.

required to fill vacancies, and residence is often a requirement for holding office.

The legislature gives school officers discretionary powers but must establish standards under which such choice may be exercised. To be binding, an order of a school officer must come from exercise of his discretion within legitimate bounds. Sometimes the law imposes upon him performance of a duty which involves no exercise of judgment; the duty is purely ministerial as distinguished from a duty which is partly "court-like" or judicial. Even though school officers are not judicial officers, the performance of their duties often requires that judgments be made. Whenever such an officer looks into the facts of a case and acts upon them, he serves in a quasi-judicial manner.

Municipal and State Officers

Two corporate entities are usually superimposed upon identical pieces of geography—civil government and the school district. The school district, however, has a separate identity from the municipality it may happen to embrace, either *in toto* or in part.

Municipal officers draw authority from both city charters and statutes, having only such powers with respect to education as are expressly delegated. In fact, when performing school functions, they are not municipal officers at all but state officers. Their functions are clearly separate from those of city officers performed under authority of municipal ordinances.

This difference in law rests upon the fact that a municipality is created voluntarily, its charter granted solely at the request of a majority of its residents. A school district is "an involuntary corporation" created without asking permission from inhabitants of the "piece of geography." The school district comprising a city can be changed only by authority of state statute, not by municipal ordinance.

School district officers. Questioning whether school officers hold office legally is the prerogative of government, not of private litigants. In other words, only state officers may prosecute an action attacking the legality of a school district. The mode of such attack is by means of "quo warranto" proceedings brought by the attorney-general in the name of the state.

Courts and state officers. It is the maintenance of the constitutional equilibrium between the several states and the federal sources of power that has brought crucial questions to the courts. The topic is broad and not altogether relevant here, save for its application to public officers.

It may be helpful to look briefly at instances in which purely negative control has been exercised by courts over officers. Such instances are those wherein acts of officers have been enjoined or restrained. In the federal courts a plaintiff may challenge an act of a state legislature on the ground of unconstitutionality. The plaintiff may seek to restrain the enforcement of an act by the state through action of state officers.[5]

The act in question may simply be one that is illegal as far as state authority is concerned. The problem is this: The state official is using the name of the state to enforce a law which is alleged to be void because of unconstitutionality. The United States Supreme Court has laid down the rule that a federal court should refrain from exercising its statutory power to enjoin state officers where the state courts are capable of affording relief. Under this broad rule, state courts, rather than federal courts, have decided that a school board is properly limited by the functions assigned to other public agencies. Here, the bases for conflict have arisen. The making of a driveway on school grounds could be considered as a function of the school district; but the constructing of a road necessary for a part of the bus route might not be considered a board function at all, since road building belongs to the state (or the county as its agent). The rule supported by the courts is that school boards are prohibited from performing functions belonging to other governmental agencies even though such functions may be needed to further public education.[6]

In summary, there are some general rules for distinguishing an employee from an officer. An employee is one who is appointed or engaged under authority to perform duties with respect to the public school system. He cannot be a public officer too. The contract term for an employee is not fixed by law or prescribed by statute. Where a person exercises none of the sovereign prerogatives of gov-

---

[5] Such procedure is within Section 266 of the United States Judicial Code, 36 Stat. 1162, 28 U.S.C.A. sec. 380.

[6] It appears that school activities are subject to control by other than school authorities under the police power of such authorities. A city Health Commission may require a board of education to procure licenses for restaurants operated by the board. A city ordinance may rightly require inspection of all public eating places. There is no encroachment here by other public agencies on board authority to manage schools.

ernment, and where duties are of a kind subject to control and direction by a school board, such a person is an employee.

A number of courts have said that the most important difference between the officer and employee is that "an employment does not authorize the exercise in one's own right of any sovereign power or any prescribed independent authority of a governmental nature."[7] The proper procedure to follow in discharging an employee is controlled by school laws rather than by general ones.[8] The distinctions between employees and officers are important because teachers would have legal rights materially affected if they were called school officers. The whole body of law dealing with public officers would then be relevant and applicable to them also.

---

[7] *State ex rel. Halloway* v. *Sheats*, 78 Fla. 583, 83 So. 508 (Fla., 1919).

[8] *Daniel* v. *Dallas Independent School District*, 351 S.W. (2d) 356 (Texas, 1961).

CHAPTER VI

Theory of Governmental Nonliability

Basis for the Doctrine

Government has been coming into greater contact with the affairs of everyone. An ever-increasing number of persons suffer injuries resulting from governmental acts and operations.[1] Damage to persons and property by agents of government has tended to increase proportionately. This rapid growth of public services by states, the large number of persons engaged in the business of education, and the increase in the number of risks brought about by the use of machines point up the need to examine the nonliability theory.

Before World War II, increasing activity by government had made acute the problems raised by the immunity theory. This doctrine holds that government cannot be held accountable in law for commission or omission of civil wrongs (torts rather than breaches of contract), regardless of the measure of culpability—unless government overtly permits itself to be "hailed into court."

In a highly technological society, accidents cause many deaths and injuries. "No school has been organized without a number of potential hazards on playgrounds, in classrooms and laboratories, on the stairs, and on the road to and from school."[2] Among children aged one to fourteen, accidents cause more deaths than disease. How much would it take to convince a court that a steam pipe exposed to passing children is a nuisance, or that provision of guard rails on retaining walls is a legal duty, or that a bus driver should make sure of no highway obstructions despite a state law requiring motorists to stop for school buses?

Accidents involving school personnel, visitors, and pupils do occur on school grounds, in corridors and on stairways, in classrooms, during athletic events, in gymnasiums and laboratories, and within shop areas. Although not technically on school premises, persons

---

[1] Frederick F. Blachly and Miriam E. Oatman, "Approaches to Governmental Liability in Tort: A Comparative Survey," *Law and Contemporary Problems,* IX (Spring, 1942), 181.

[2] Willard E. Givens, "Pupil Patrols in Elementary and Secondary Schools," *Research Bulletin,* XXVIII, National Education Association (February, 1950), 4.

may be injured on field trips, which are usually considered to be a part of the school curriculum.[3] Although school personnel may regard themselves as faultless toward those who sustain injuries from "engaging in school activities," court cases arise regularly in which school personnel are named as defendants.

From the viewpoint of the injured, against whom can he proceed to recover damages? Who is liable for injury because of the negligent conduct of school persons? From whom may visitors injured on school premises recover? Answers require delving into concepts such as "liability," "school districts as a part of "government," and "immunity." The word "liability" in *Black's Law Dictionary* is "the state of being bound or obligated in law or justice to do, pay, or make good something." As a part of government, a school district cannot be sued without consent of government. Exemption from suit in tort renders it "immune" from liability for injury directly or indirectly suffered by others.

A school district enjoys immunity because it is an agency of government, created to carry out a state function. In any school-associated accident, the injured party (except in a few states) is without a remedy. This is so even if the school district itself is responsible for the harm done. The obstacle in the way of redress is the immunity doctrine. The rule is that the injured party cannot obtain judgment against a school district for injury traceable to its negligent acts.

Origins.   The English idea of irresponsibility of government for injury to citizens appears to be the outgrowth of historical events and circumstances.[4] Origins can be traced to feudal times. The idea is found in political theory developed under the "divine right" concept. Two writers on the problem of governmental liability for tort have stated:

> The doctrine that sovereignty is the highest power of the state, that it is subject to no law, but is itself the creator of law, and that it resides in the monarch, did much to place the state in a position of irresponsibility for its torts. . . .[5]

As reasons to justify the theory, courts have said (1) that school districts should not be charged with liability since they receive no advantage from operating schools; (2) that school districts have

---

[3] It would be well for school personnel to insist that the board of education include within its written policy a definition of "school curriculum" broad enough to encompass instructional activities away from the school campus itself.

[4] Blachly and Oatman, *Law and Contemporary Problems*, p. 182.

[5] *Ibid.*, p. 183.

only those powers given them by the legislature and state school officers, not including permission to commit legal errors; (3) that school taxes are trust funds, not to be used to pay claims; (4) that school property is exempt from attachment; and (5) that the personal interest of private citizens must give way to the idea of public good.[6]

Thus, the injured citizen cannot sue his state, at least in most jurisdictions. Based upon a doctrine that sovereigns cannot be subjected to litigation, the theory prevents suit in most jurisdictions. To make government liable, the legislature must upset the doctrine. The greatest number of school districts operate in states where this bit of the common law remains intact.

The doctrine prevails with strict application in most states, despite modifications. Some statutes have authorized suits against the state or its subdivisions by all persons having claims against them. Courts, however, have interpreted such enactments as merely permitting the filing of suits or claims and not affecting the substantive liability of government.

Criticisms.   There is dissatisfaction with a rule that school districts (or other agencies of government operating public schools) are immune from suit for tort. Even though it has crescendoed since 1945, criticism started as long ago as 1793. At that time the United States Supreme Court was not able to find sovereign immunity in the federal Constitution. Almost 70 years later, Lincoln said that it is as much the duty of government to render proper justice against itself, in favor of its citizens, as to administer the same between private individuals.

Within a generation after Lincoln's pronouncement, the United States Supreme Court said:

> . . . while the exemption of the United States and of the several states from being subjected as defendants to ordinary actions in the courts has since that time been repeatedly asserted here, the principle has never been discussed or the reasons for it given, but it has always been treated as an established doctrine.[7]

After World War I, the English Parliament merely considered a bill that would have (1) placed the Crown almost in the same position as the subject with reference to power to sue and be sued;

---

[6] Madaline Kinter Remmlein, "Tort Liability of School Districts, Boards, and Employees," in *Law and the School Business Manager,* ed. Garber (Danville, Ill.: Interstate Printers and Publishers, Inc., 1957), p. 195.

[7] *United States* v. *Lee,* 106 U.S. 196, 207 (1882).

(2) made the Crown liable to be sued in tort; and (3) made it possible for the Crown to recover and pay costs as a subject litigant.[8]

Since 1945, criticism of the concept has steadily mounted. Committees of the American Bar Association and of the American Political Science Association have studied various aspects of the broad subject. Legal scholars and political scientists have judged most of the relaxations of sovereign immunity (both legislative and judicial) to be only fragmentary and to allow many occasions for injustice to continue.[9]

A former law school dean has been a leader in denouncing the immunity theory and has dubbed it "a relic of the Dark Ages." Judges have criticized the theory. However, those who have attacked the doctrine have usually followed precedents laid down under the theory. Despite this rule, one court boldly stated:

> . . . The errors of history, logic, and policy which were responsible for the development of this concept have been clearly exposed, and thoroughly criticized. Nevertheless, the solution of the problem of governmental responsibility in tort is too complex an undertaking to permit the partial and piecemeal judicial reform which the plaintiff seeks. Establishment of a comprehensive program by legislation applicable to the Commonwealth and to all its subdivisions is sorely needed to deal effectively with tort claims arising out of the conduct of governmental activities.[10]

The next year, the Illinois Supreme Court overturned the doctrine.[11] It said that the doctrine rested upon "a rotten foundation."

In the decade of the 1960's, efforts continue by politicians, judges, lawyers, and the public to break down the rule. The Michigan Supreme Court, in commenting on a tort case, said that the single question on appeal was whether the state would continue to adhere to governmental immunity from torts. It said: "From this date forward the judicial doctrine of governmental immunity from ordinary torts no longer exists. . . ."

---

[8] Blachly and Oatman, *Law and Contemporary Problems,* p. 184.

[9] From the "Foreword," Blachly and Oatman, *Law and Contemporary Problems.*

[10] *Morris* v. *School District of Township of Mount Lebanon,* 144 A. (2d) 737 (Pa., 1958). Here the school district was held liable for the death of a child participating in its summer recreation program.

[11] *Molitor* v. *Kaneland Community Unit District No. 302,* 163 N.E. (2d) 89 Illinois, 1959). The Illinois Supreme Court argued that it was incredible that, in this modern age, medieval absolutism should exempt various branches of government from their liability for torts. The Court stated that the community, not the individual, should bear the responsibility for loss.

The feeling grows that a person injured by government should be able to look to government for redress, just as he could do if he were to sue privately. Many agree that a state should be held responsible for damages in a tort action where the state (or its duly chosen agents) knowingly permits a dangerous and hazardous condition to continue to exist without proper safeguards and warnings. When government ignores danger, this fact alone should be sufficient to place responsibility upon it.

The Federal Tort Claims Act of 1945 represented a real stride by government toward the assumption of complete tort liability. In addition to statute, there are indirect methods by which tort liability of government is created. Some are subtle or concealed and are therefore easy to overlook.

Some wonder whether the states could enact a kind of statute which would say: "The State of X recognizes and assumes the compassionate responsibility of the State for the loss sustained by reason of the acts of its agents." Half the states now have statutes providing for municipal liability for mob damage—sometimes irrespective of fault.

There are no easy solutions to liability problems. In fact, there are more questions than answers. For example, how should claims against the state and its agents be handled?[12] How should government meet such obligations? Also, what is an adequate plan for protecting officers and employees in the performance of governmental duties? Can one system of responsibility be established which is applicable to all levels of government? Any complete discussion of governmental responsibility for injuries involves these concerns, as well as the nature of the state and decisions about what are ethical bases for the establishment of responsibility.[13]

Disagreements will continue, because the doctrine of governmental immunity is not equitable under modern conditions. Thus, legislatures and courts will proceed to find ways around the obstacle, for deviations to avoid the concept have become habit. Some legal scholars feel that the theory is definitely on the wane. The doctrine has markedly less prestige now than it formerly had. Legislation modeled after the Federal Tort Claims Act will be urged in the legislatures of the 50 United States during the 1960's and 1970's.

---

[12] Blachly and Oatman, *Law and Contemporary Problems,* p. 181.
[13] *Ibid.,* p. 181.

Negligence Theory

Some understanding of the principles on which negligence rests is essential to understand the legal basis for much litigation. Actions of employees and officers of government are interpreted by the courts in light of the nature of negligence. What kind of conduct (behavior) constitutes negligence "in terms of legal standards" to make a person responsible to another for damages?

Under the legal system of the United States—based upon the English Common Law rather than Continental law—every person enjoys the right to be free from bodily injury, intentionally or carelessly caused by others. Any measure of carelessness indicates neglect, ignorance, or mistake. Negligence is any conduct which falls below the standard established by law for the protection of others against unreasonable harm. Five elements must appear in order to subject a defendant to liability for negligence: (1) The law protects from unintentional invasions the interest alleged by the plaintiff; (2) the actor is negligent with respect to the protected interest; (3) the actor's conduct is the legal cause of invasion; (4) plaintiff has suffered damages as a result of defendant's invasion of plaintiff's protected interest; and (5) plaintiff has conducted himself so as to enable him to bring an action for such invasion.[14]

Negligent conduct is of two types: (1) There are acts which a prudent man should realize involve an unreasonable risk of injury to others. (2) There are failures to do an act which is necessary to protect another and which one is under legal duty to do. To clarify further:

> An act of negligence may be one which involves unreasonable risk of harm to others, even though it is done with reasonable care, skill, preparation, and warning. The negligence is inherent in the act. In other types of conduct, the act may become negligent through the lack of care, skill, preparation, or warning, although the act in itself would not have constituted negligent conduct had reasonable care, skill, preparation, or warning been used.[15]

---

[14] These five elements, according to Ludwig Teller, *National Law Review Series-Torts* (New York: Harmon Publications, 1948), p. 45, are the nuclei about which the whole law of negligence revolves. Moreover, he states these must be considered in logical sequence. The question of contributory negligence cannot possibly arise until it is determined that the defendant has been guilty of negligence. To go back still further, a case should not be allowed to progress to the state where negligence becomes an issue, unless it be found that the plaintiff has an interest which the law protects.

[15] NEA, "Who Is Liable for Pupil Injuries?" National Commission on Safety Education (February, 1963), p. 11.

In deciding whether negligence exists, courts consider the nature of the conduct, legal cause of injury, and foreseeability of harm.

Definition.   Negligence is a relation among things. A duty to use diligence exists and may be owed to one person and not to another. Centering on failure to exercise care, the negligence question is: "Did the defendant use such care as ordinarily prudent men would use under similar circumstances?" Whether the facts involve negligence is a question the jury decides under instructions from the court. The judge informs the jury of matters of law as a part of such instruction. Negligence law does not exist in a vacuum; it must be a balance of interests.

One defense against negligence is alleging "contributory negligence." This is conduct by the injured plaintiff which falls below the standard to which he should conform for his own protection and which is legally a contributing cause. A plaintiff's contributory negligence bars recovery against an otherwise liable defendant. If a school employee is guilty of intentional wrong, he may not invoke the doctrine of contributory fault to relieve himself of liability.

The duty of care in rendering services performed gratuitously is different from contractual situations. A potential defendant is not liable where the relationship is nonbusiness. The function of law, states Teller, is negative rather than affirmative.[16] It specifies minimum standards only and permits one to act at that level. It is not the purpose of law to coerce the existence of "good Samaritans." The law cannot determine whether refusal to render aid was based upon physical or mental shortcomings rather than upon callous indifference to others.

Tort liabilities.   Liability is determined by the negligence of the one who is the "legal cause" of the injury. In a tort action, recovery is predicated upon the breach of a legal duty owed by defendant to plaintiff. The legal cause of injury then is "that cause among all the antecedent events which, without interference of an independent superseding cause, produced the damage." Between the wrongful act and the injury, there must have been an unbroken connection. The sequence must have been such as to make it equitable to hold the defendant responsible. If conduct of one person is a substantial factor in bringing about injury to another, and if there is no rule relieving him of liability, that person's negligence is the legal cause of the injury.

---

[16] Teller, *National Law Review Series—Torts*, p. 55.

Courts are not concerned with humane sides of the questions. The omission or negligent discharge of "legal duties" only is within the court's sphere of concern. The difficulty lies in proving the legal cause—that cause *but for which* the person would not have been injured. In cases involving recklessness, a jury is more apt to construe the element of causation in favor of the plaintiff than in a case of simple carelessness only.

Nuisance as negligence. Harboring a nuisance is another theory on which some courts have assigned liability to school districts. A restricted definition of nuisance is "some activity on land which damages the property of others situated outside the limits of the land." Some examples of nuisances are (1) maintaining a flagpole in an unsafe condition; (2) discharging sewage into a stream; and (3) maintaining defective sanitary facilities on school property.

Things which are not liked are not automatically nuisances, however. At common law, a person cannot press for an action in tort for a nuisance, even though he has sustained harm, *unless* he can demonstrate that he has sustained a particular injury. The facts alleged may not constitute an actionable nuisance. If the plaintiff can show that he is privately damaged by a public nuisance, he may recover in a civil action. Nuisance may become descriptive of some harm done rather than of a type of legal duty owed. Continuance of invasion of private rights is often the distinction between nuisance and negligence.

The legal status of one who is injured is also important in connection with nuisance. The general rule is nonliability for injury suffered by an adult trespasser—one who violates willfully and forcibly the rights of another. The rule, however, does not apply to an infant trespasser when circumstances bring the case within the "attractive nuisance doctrine." This doctrine imposes liability when a dangerous instrumentality is easily accessible to children of "tender years."

The "turntable" doctrine holds a property owner liable for injury when he "knowingly leaves a dangerous instrumentality . . . exposed in a place liable to be frequented by children, as a result of which a child who because of his tenders years did not realize the danger, is injured."[17] Courts apply the doctrine where the danger is extreme and where it is maintained close to places frequented by the public.

---

[17] *Ibid.,* pp. 67–68.

School District Liability

That "education is a function of the state" needs no amplification. It is relevant here (even if obvious) since most states adhere to the principle of governmental immunity where the sovereign has been attacked on account of injury to person or property. This principle applies to state activity and that of its agents, such as school districts. The fundamental rule is that a school district is not liable for damages resulting from its own negligence or that of its agents or employees, when that district performs a duty imposed on it by law. However, such law may explicitly provide exception to the common law rule. California and New York have made sweeping alterations in statutes.

With the exception of those states where the immunity rule has been altered by statute, school districts are protected from liability in criminal and tort law. To be thus sheltered, they must not have engaged in active or positive wrongdoing, as opposed to mere acts of negligence.

Exceptions to the rule. The rule is that an agency of government—such as a board of education—is liable when it commits a nuisance. Falling short of overturning the immunity rule, courts have seized upon this exception to the doctrine to hold that permanent and dangerous conditions constitute a nuisance. Where the courts so rule, the injured person may recover damages. In addition, efforts to obtain relief from the unyielding application of the immunity rule have been made through the "differentiation of function" idea. Attempts are made to hold a school district liable on the ground that the injury complained of was incurred as the result of participation by the district in a proprietary function, as opposed to a governmental one. When injury arises out of a function that is profit motivated, the immunity rule, affords no protection.

The rules, however, persist. Thus, boards of education have the responsibility to see that pupils enrolled (and those invited to school premises) are provided with a safe environment. One court has stated that it is doubtful that a governmental body such as a board of education "can entertain a malicious intent." This may be true. However, when ice is on the walkway which must be taken by invitees, the danger is foreseeable. A school board owes the public reasonable and ordinary care.

Good faith policy. When a board acts in good faith by following current law, no liability attaches. A board can make and pass any rule which is reasonable, providing it lies within its jurisdiction. Within such scope, rules and regulations are legislation having legal force equal to state board regulations and state statutes. When a board attempts to enforce an unreasonable rule, it invites trouble. Recourse may be had to the courts on the part of injured parties.

Legislative intent. Legislators intend that their provisions will act as shields to defend the rights of people who have a legitimate claim against an agency of the state. Negligence may be predicated on the violation of a duty prescribed in the statutes, provided the intent of the statute is to protect individuals rather than the public in general. However, it is not necessary that the statute provide for civil liability.

A statute may be worded to intend to create an interest in an individual, the violation of which will subject the violator to a civil action for damages at the instance of the injured plaintiff. There is some logic to support this principle. Statute law is a matter of public record, and any part is conceded to be a portion of the whole. A knowledge of it must be imputed to everybody. Every person is presumed to know the law, even though the law is of great magnitude. Could it be otherwise? If we could plead ignorance of some parts of the law, the court would have to spend endless hours questioning and testing as to precisely what part of the law the defendant did know. Administrative rules and regulations however, are not as popularly understood as statute law.

Despite statutes, legislative intent, and constitutional restrictions, the question still persists: Have the courts begun to recognize the possibility of liability of the school district, even though it is not specifically imposed by law? As of 1963, the courts in three states had placed on school districts the legal responsibility for torts without prior statutory imposition of liability. The courts thus acted in Illinois, New York, and Wisconsin. The Minnesota Supreme Court went on record that, after 1963, it would not recognize governmental immunity as a defense to tort claims against school districts.

Insurance. Pupils and school employees should be protected from injury, and the board seems to be the logical protector. However, if the board is expected to assume responsibility, it should also be provided with protection. The jump is not far to the matter of insurance and related compensation for injuries suffered by third parties at the provocation of the school.

Does liability insurance coverage help compensate the person injured on school premises? If the person is injured within a school district that has purchased liability insurance, but where state law contains no waiver of governmental immunity to the limits of the policy, under prevailing court opinion the injured party is unable to proceed against such school district. Even if the person wishes only to establish his claim in order to recover from the insurance company, he may not do so. If, on the other hand, an injured party lives in a state that empowers and authorizes school boards specifically to purchase liability insurance to cover the district for negligence, and if the district has so procured such insurance coverage, the injured person may be able to collect damages up to the coverage in the policy.

Under liability insurance, payments for damages to the injured person depend upon the negligence of the insured—that is, carelessness of the school district (or of the covered school personnel). Accident-type insurance is payable regardless of fault. The feature of such a policy is that it provides for compensation to the injured based on accident, not due to the negligence of the insured.

To protect innocent persons from the negligence of school boards, citizens should get the law amended to permit suits against school districts where there is insurance coverage. The chances of collecting damages by an injured person from the insuror are enhanced if the authorizing law provides that the governmental immunity doctrine is waived to the extent of the insurance purchased. The law should be clear that the insurance company is the one to be sued and that it may not assert, as a defense to payment, the governmental immunity doctrine.

The purpose of strict adherence to the immunity rule by courts, even when insurance is in force, would seem to be one of prudence. A liability policy is not issued primarily for the protection of the insured, but for the protection of the public. It is they who must be saved from thoughtless behavior which, but for the protection of such insurance funds, would make it possible to expend earmarked education dollars to pay damage claims. Even the tort liability laws of the several states do not "create liability" or "causes of action." They merely limit the amount of damages if and when liability is imposed by a court. The contention abounds that a defendant school district "has always had immunity from tort liability." What it has "always had" is immunity from collectibility of judgment in proper circumstances, not immunity from suit itself. Liability, of and by itself, depends not merely upon the collectibility of the judgment, but upon the presence of nontrust funds. To overcome the barrier of governmental immunity from tort liability, a complaint against a school district must allege the existence of such "unearmarked" funds (for example, liability insurance dollars).

Informed persons suggest that the "doctrine of immunity" be laid to rest once and for all. A school district must be held liable for its own negligent acts. Obstacles, however, may be formidable. What effect, for example, would abrogation have on board employees? Would board employees hesitate to venture beyond the classroom walls? How much of the board employee's time would be consumed by litigation? Would new kinds of friction arise between boards and the public? Between employees and parents? Would school employees suffer any new kind of stigma? Perhaps litigation would increase so much that school districts would be eventually forced to abandon the public schools to nonpublic corporations.

CHAPTER VII

Liability of Individual
Members of a Board

The immunity rule pertains to the liability of board members as well as to the school board itself. As an individual, however, a board member may incur liability for his own torts. These may involve improper negotiations, overstepping his discretionary powers, and failure to carry out a purely ministerial act.

No action can be successfully maintained against a school officer (and a board member is such an officer) when he acts without malice. A board member acting without malice is shielded further by the distinction between types of liability. Legal accountability for the exercise of discretion is quite different from liability imposed for acting negligently. Members of a board, for example, are not held liable in their individual capacities for the negligent operation of district's school buses. One court in 1954 found no evidence that bus operation was such as to amount to malicious, willful, and wanton conduct on the part of board members as individuals.[1]

General Nonliability Principle

A board member is not held personally liable for injuries growing out of errors in judgment, however great these might be. As long as the school official acts honestly, in good faith, and within his proper jurisdiction, he escapes liability. He must, however, act within the scope of the corporate powers of the board to avoid the possibility of legal involvement.

An old case illustrates still another principle: that no liability attaches when a board member erroneously exercises actual power rather than assumes power for an act not warranted at all.[2] Acting in good faith and without fraud, a board member will not be held personally liable on contracts. This is so even though it should be

---

[1] *Krasner* v. *Harper,* 90 Ga. App. 128, 82 S.E. (2d) 267 (1954).
[2] *Sweeney* v. *Young,* 82 N.H. 159, 131 Atl. 155, 42 A.L.R. 757 (1925).

discovered that—through mistake of the law—the school officer has exceeded the authority conferred upon him by statute.

Moreover, it is the governing board itself which is responsible if there is district liability. In other words, liability ordinarily attaches to the unit, not to the members. A board resembles a private corporation. Such boards act "as a unit" with individual members losing identity as separate persons. No single member has a legal right to take independent action regarding school affairs. The sole exception is that the whole board may delegate to one or several members, authority to perform some particular act for the board itself.[3] Being an arm of state government, a school board acts for the people within the scope of power delegated by the state constitution, statutes, and pertinent rules and regulations. When a school officer enters into a contract with respect to matters committed to his charge, it is always presumed that he intended to bind the district and not himself, and that parties dealing with him did not rely upon his personal responsibility.

Some Bases for Liability

The principle which applies to tort actions brought against school districts is not under consideration here. This principle applies to tort actions brought against a board member who acts as an agent for the board itself. Some school laws make individual board members personally liable for violations of such laws. The failure to carry out mandatory legal provisions ordinarily imposes personal liability, for "where the law is plain and mandatory, there can be no exercise of discretion."

When the law imposes a duty upon a person which he refuses or fails to perform, he is answerable in damages to those who may be injured by such failure. A duty is ministerial (as opposed to quasi-judicial) when the law imposes upon a public officer performance of a duty involving no exercise of judgment. He must perform such an act and do so in a proper manner. The legislature alone prescribes standards by statute. Once passed, a statute cannot be altered according to the whim of any officer.

The performance of many duties by school officers requires the exercise of judgment. In such exercise, the danger of board liability is necessarily present. There may be individual liability if and when a board member misuses tax funds. A public officer is an

---

[3] Remmlein, in *Law and the School Business Manager*, p. 193.

insurer of public funds lawfully in his possession. He is therefore liable, even for losses which may occur. He is legally answerable, and liability is absolute, except for those acts of nature, or the public enemy.

There may be individual liability if a board member makes a personal gain from a public contract. Also, members of the board may be held personally liable if a board purchases real property without the authority of the electors of the district, or if the board lets a contract without obtaining competitive bids. In order for liability to attach to acts of individuals, they must have violated mandatory legal prescriptions. A board member may not sell or deliver an article which he knows to be inherently dangerous. Otherwise, he is responsible, aside from any contractual relation, to all persons reasonably to be expected to use the article. A board member must not attempt to enforce an unconstitutional statute. When he does, he is proceeding without authority, and his actions do not affect the state in its sovereign capacity. Because his act was illegal, the officer is stripped of his official character and is subjected in his person to the consequences of his individual conduct. In short, government does not have the power to protect a state official when he acts illegally.

Liability arises only if a board member uses language that expressly binds himself or pledges himself as the responsible party in any negotiations. If a member conceals, mistakes, or misrepresents his authority, there may be fraud in inducing others to bargain. When a board member clearly assumes personal liability, he is personally bound. It makes no difference that the business entered into was beyond the power of the board itself.

To summarize, every official act of a public officer is accompanied with the presumption of legality. Usually, nothing short of willful misconduct subjects an officer to liability for acts done in the exercise of his official discretion. This is especially so where the school official has violated no positive law. To be on the side of prudence, however, a board member should name himself as a member of a board when he individually signs a contract for the board of education. The school district should be named as the contracting party. Each signer should include his own title under his signature.

A board officer is not usually liable for his acts of nonfeasance or for school employees' acts of misfeasance, unless he participated in such acts directly. He is always liable for a personal act of misfeasance committed against another, even though such act occurred in the discharge of his public duties. The law affords no immunity from willful wrongs or malicious acts. Always, a school board member may be held personally liable for intentional torts committed while administering the affairs of the school districts.

CHAPTER VIII

Personal Liability of School Employees

There is as much likelihood of an employee's running afoul of the law in the matter of pupil accidents as on any other one point. Although some incidents causing injury or death result from pure accidents, others stem from wrongful conduct on the part of (1) principals, (2) teachers, (3) other school personnel, and (4) pupils themselves. Estimates of school-involved lawsuits give the number as being higher than 6,000 per year. One or more persons in these school suits sought money damages amounting to more than twelve million dollars. Jury dollar awards come directly out of pockets of taxpayers, and are being rendered with increasing frequency. The irreparable losses, though, are the intangibles rather than dollars— the lowered teacher morale, neglected children, and impaired school programs.

Extent of Liability

The question of teacher liability arises most frequently in connection with injuries to pupils. Legal accountability is involved in such matters as trips to Washington, class parties held outside of school hours, pupils who arrive early at school and remain late because of bus schedules. What constitutes adequate playground supervision by a teacher during school recesses, at noon hour, and before and after school hours? Should the board of education be permitted to provide liability insurance for every pupil, or accident insurance for employees of the type offered to individuals on a voluntary basis?

From previous sections, it will be recalled that a tort is a wrong committed against the person or property of another. Independent of contract, a tort is a breach of duty which the law imposes. It may be the commission or omission of an act by means of which another receives some injury—directly or indirectly. Tort liability refers to responsibility placed by the law upon one when he commits a wrong against person, property, or reputation. He must answer to the one injured, often by payment of money damages. In

98

torts, the stress is not the intent behind the act. Rather, it stresses damage done to an injured party. Reimbursement paid by a defendant is called "damages." This is the financial responsibility he must assume.

No person worthy of the name "teacher" would purposely harm a child. However, when a pupil is injured, the teacher may be at fault. There is no concern here about a child's criminal acts to which neither a parent or teacher is a party. Within the narrower concern of "torts," reported cases make much of ideas like malice, fraud, intent, and negligence. Actually, the responsibility for torts —including intentionl wrongs and plain carelessness—comes down to this simple question: When should a man be liable for harm he does to others?

Here, concern is limited to teachers as school employees when the employing board is not liable. The question is asked since "accidents" or "mistakes" may involve many types of teachers. For example, teachers of shop and physical education courses are vulnerable because of the dangerous nature of the activities. These instructors are obligated to warn pupils by oral admonition, by posted warnings, and by employing close supervision. Safety devices must be checked, and unauthorized pupils must be kept away from dangerous equipment.

A shop teacher owes a high duty of care to his own pupils—those regularly enrolled in courses in which he is the teacher. He owes merely ordinary care to those who request permission to use equipment for merely private purposes.

The liability of teachers of physical education is no greater than for other teachers, but opportunities for injury are greater. Injuries may result from falls from horizontal ladders and from gymnastics. Some injuries involve defective or inadequate gymnasium equipment, and pupils are sometimes hurt in boxing matches.

A visitor to any part of the school premises, including the shops and gymnasium, has a right to expect that the premises which he visits will be in a reasonably safe condition. But he may only expect (or should only expect) such protection if he stays within that part of the premises which he necessarily must use to carry out the purpose of his visit to the school. If injury results, a teacher cannot disclaim liability for his negligence on the ground that all teachers know no better. The standard of care in law is based upon present conditions of educational knowledge, not upon past conditions acquiesced to by others.

To the athletic coach, obvious dangers are injuries to participants as a result of improper practice. Injuries may result from players' tackling defective "dummies." Participants may be injured in so-called "touch" football skirmishes. Pupils may be hurt on the athletic field and in the stadium. Sometimes, an injury occurs as a result of club initiations. Any teacher knows that injuries may result from objects thrown. A lead pencil has caused injury. Pieces from broken milk bottles may cut pupils.

The teacher may be actively careless. Pupils have been injured when sent to poke up fires in "pot-bellied" stoves. They have been hurt by moving pianos that they have been requested to help move. Children have been injured by falls from chairs on which they stood to water classroom plants. A boy's finger became infected as a result of a teacher's holding it in boiling water.

School accidents result from collisions of bicycles and children or into walls when the teacher is "on duty." A scooter may run into a school bus and cause serious injuries. Injury results from pushing and shoving while pupils wait in bus lines. It may result from disciplinary measures taken when "incorrigibles" try the patience and restraint of their teachers.

An injured person wants recovery. When harmed by a school employee or pupil, he can always seek redress from the individual personally responsible for negligently causing the injury, whether that individual be a teacher, administrator, bus driver, any other employee, or merely a fellow pupil. This is so because private individuals are ordinarily personally responsible if their own negligence results in injuries to persons within the school. This liability exists just as though a nonschool person had been injured.

The above details are not intended to scare teachers and students from the profession or, out of sheer panic, into purchasing "mountains of liability insurance." However, the teacher who held the small boy's infected finger in boiling water for several minutes was obviously liable for damages resulting from the tort. This was not an ordinarily prudent person, against which the courts judge men's actions.

Ordinary Care Theory

The courts have said that a teacher is bound to exercise that care which a parent of ordinary prudence would exercise under comparable circumstances. Here is the direct application of the doctrine that the teacher stands *in loco parentis* to the pupil. The obligation to be reasonably prudent exists in the classroom and on the playgrounds and fields. If injuries result to a pupil as a direct result of a teacher's failure to show that care, the teacher is personally liable. He cannot escape by trying to shift the legal burden to the nonliable school district.

Lack of proper supervision is one circumstance held by courts to make a teacher personally liable for pupil injury. There seems to be increasing disposition for juries to return verdicts for substantial amounts. The underlying principle is: A teacher may be held personally liable for injuries directly or proximately sustained by pupils under the teacher's care and resulting from the teacher's negligence or failure of duty.

"What is "ordinary care" poses some debate. It may be argued, for example, that humans are empyric and subjective as a matter of fact. Consequently, no standard of care can exist apart from one's own experience. The law, however, is properly otherwise. The reason is that men are apt to be more objective when the conduct of "reasonable men" is held forth as the legal test. The invitor owes the duty of ordinary care to his guest. He is under the duty of having in a reasonably safe condition those parts of his premises to which invitees come. Even when the presence of a trespasser becomes known (one who has no business at all on school premises), an obligation arises to exercise care in the doing of acts otherwise lawful, if the trespasser would be subjected to possible injury.

The juryman decides the question of due care by not using himself as a criterion, but by considering what an ordinary person would do under the circumstances. Any other charge by the court is subject to reversal on appeal. Standards of care may be defined in fairly precise ways, since certain situations occur with such frequency that courts are inclined to take a definite stand to fix a standard of care in all such cases. Custom may be considered in determining whether sufficient care has been exercised. However, it is not conclusive or controlling, because the customary way of doing a thing may be the negligent way, creating a false standard. A fundamental test of whether a person has a cause of action in tort against another is this: Did the person who is the defendant owe a duty to do something he did not do, or owe a duty not to do something he did do?

Court cases plainly state that in order for a negligent actor to be held liable for the plaintiff's injury, it is necessary that the negligence of the actor be a legal cause of another's harm. The conduct of the actor must be a "substantial factor" in bringing out the harm for which a suit is brought. Two elements must be present for a teacher to be liable for another's bodily harm. It is necessary (1) that the teacher's conduct be negligent toward the other—that is, be below the standard of care imposed by the court; and (2) that the lack of care must be the legal cause of the other's harm.

When in the judgment of the court a "reasonably prudent" person could have foreseen the harmful consequences of his behavior, the actor becomes liable for negligent conduct in disregarding these foreseeable outcomes. The test of "foreseeability" is important as a positive precaution also. When faced with a lawsuit, the teacher is not at fault if he can demonstrate that he planned well and ahead of time for the particular event. This can mean many things. Even though of no legal consequence in taking away from minors their right to sue, permission slips do show that planning was involved. In addition, teachers' associations should request, through the superintendent's office, that the board of education define in the official policies a concept of curriculum broad enough to include activities away from the school campus.

Types of Actions

Criminal responsibility of the school employee is something different from the problem of personal liability for tort. There are "absolute duties" which relate to criminal law enforcement and which exist independent of legal rights. Relative duties pertain to civil law enforcement and correspond to legal rights. When a person is entitled to a certain right, others are subject to a corresponding duty. Criminal liability is involved when a person knowingly permits an act of hazing, injuring, frightening, or degrading of a school pupil; if he knowingly diverts school funds to any use or purpose other than that for which it was raised or appropriated; if he is interested in a contract for the purchase of property, supplies, or fire insurance for the use of the board with which he is legally related; if he accepts, offers, or agrees to receive a reward, consideration, present, gift, or price reduction in reference to the sale or use of textbooks or school supplies; or if he refuses to perform his duties under the compulsory education law.

Automobile-Induced Litigation

The social and legal problems attendant upon dangers involved in the use of automobiles caused the enactment of the vehicle and traffic laws which provide for a wide range of contingencies. In substance, most such laws state that

> ... every owner of a motor vehicle operated upon a public highway shall be liable and responsible for death or injuries to person or property resulting from negligence in the operating of such motor vehicle in the business of such owner or otherwise, by any person legally using or operating the same.[1]

Guest statutes. In about half the states, there are so-called "guest statutes" which protect the teacher-driver from suits by persons conveyed gratuitously. If the driver is grossly negligent, however, he is liable. The law treats the guest, invited into the host's automobile, in the same manner as it treats the gratuitous licensee or social guests on land. Here the landowner's liability serves as an example for that of the automobile owner—at least with respect to the condition of the auto itself.

The rule is that the guest must accept the vehicle as he finds it. The host is under no legal duty to exercise care to discover and repair defects not known to him. However, if a teacher lends his auto to a friend without disclosing a defect known to him, that teacher is subject to liability in case of injury. He is liable not only to his friend, but also to anyone whom his friend permits to drive the car, or whom the friend chooses to receive in it as passenger or guest. This is provided, of course, that it was understood between the parties that the car could so be used.

The one being transported is not a guest within the meaning of guest statutes if he pays either a fixed sum or his share of the car expense. The teacher-driver would be liable for ordinary negligence, since this is the driver's responsibility toward all passengers where no guest statute exists. If the teacher who thus drives his own car has "extended coverage" on it, that policy would protect him and any other person using the car with the teacher-owner's permission.

That a guest agrees to pay a share of expenses of a motor trip does not establish a "joint enterprise" or a paying-passenger relationship. Mere contributions to expenses have not been construed

---

[1] Stated in Teller, *National Law Review Series—Torts,* p. 82.

as payment for transportation but as acts of courtesy.[2] One case was that of a 15-year-old boy who was permitted by the owner to drive the auto with the owner as passenger. Here because of a principal-agent relationship, the boy's negligence was imputed to the owner.[3] Where a driver was using the plaintiff's automobile to serve his own interests and was not engaged upon a mission for the plaintiff, either as agent or employee, negligence of the driver of the plaintiff's automobile could not be imputed to the plaintiff to bar recovery for damage to the automobile.[4]

Degree of care. Aside from driver-passenger problems, a motorist must exercise a high degree of care in the presence of children on or near a public highway. A motorist's degree of care is diminished when a child is accompanied by an adult. A teacher-motorist who entered an intersection on a green light had no legal duty to turn his head to look either way. No motorist is the insurer of the safety of those who project themselves into his pathway. He is charged, however, with responsibility for having his vehicle under control at all times and for maintaining an attentive outlook in order to meet an emergency within reason, consistent with reasonable caution. A court said that a 9-year-old boy could rely on the prudence of the bus driver and approaching motorists.[5] Considering age, experience, and surrounding circumstances, the court held that the boy was not contributorily negligent when he was struck by an automobile while attempting to cross a street after alighting from the bus.

Employees should check details carefully before using personal automobiles for school-connected events. Legal danger in this area is substantial. If a court finds negligence, the teacher-driver will be personally liable. In some states, the school district would also be held liable. Failure to employ care not to harm others spells negligence. An employee should not use his or anybody else's automobile without first seeing that he has his current driver's license

---

[2] The complaint alleged that the defendant had agreed to take the plaintiff along on a trip in consideration for plaintiff's paying certain expenses. Court stated this was insufficient to allege a nonguest status. See *Minnick* v. *Keene*, 139 So. (2d) 172 (Fla., 1962).

[3] In *Service Fire Insurance Company* v. *Johnson*, 139 So. (2d) 410 (La., 1962), the court said that the boy's negligence, with respect to a collision while the auto was on the wrong side of the road, was imputable to the owner. Here, the owner had a theoretical right of control over the driver since he was a passenger in his own car and the trip was for his own benefit.

[4] *Washington Fire & Marine Insurance Company* v. *Bacon*, 138 So. (2d) 667 (La., 1962).

[5] *Gaspard* v. *Lemaire*, 146 So. (2d) 467 (La., 1962).

with him. If he is a newcomer, he must make sure that his new state permits a nonresident to drive for 90 days without getting a temporary permit. He must determine whether insurance of the owner of a vehicle covers a driver who is alone but who has received the permission of the auto owner to use it.

Field trips.   It is an unusual teacher who has never remarked, "Children, tomorrow we will take a field trip." What responsibility does a teacher have for children on such a trip? Discussion among teachers centers about the methods they and others can use to prevent suits for damages. It is not unusual for employees to cancel trips because a parent informed the school that he would sue in case of injury to his child.

For field trips, more than ordinary care should be taken in planning properly. The principal and teachers should make reasonable rules governing pupils who attend events away from school. They may enforce such regulations in the same way as they would enforce classroom rules. The teacher should take pupils only in small groups.

Teachers should avoid assuming the responsibility for conducting pupils through an industrial plant. They should remember that the plant owners have no duty of care to licensees who are there purely for their own benefit. Adequate supervision under such circumstances is seldom good enough. The employees in charge could act in a reasonably prudent manner and display at least an average amount of foresight and concern for the pupils in their charge; yet, they would fall short because of the very nature of the premises.

Some suggestions to follow are: (1) Get the permission of parents before the trip. (2) Secure enough qualified supervisors. (3) Investigate thoroughly the particular hazards of the place to be visited. (4) Urge the board of education to accept trips as part and parcel of the educational program. Having obtained permission from home is important, if not a legal excuse, when injury occurs. Waivers signed by parents do not relieve school employees of any possible liability for pupil injuries on field trips. The difficulty is that a parent may not legally sign away the rights of his child to collect damages in the event of injury due to negligence. In other words, a school employee cannot escape the penalty for his own negligence even when a parent voluntarily waives his right to sue for damages.

Unavoidable accident.   In using motor vehicles, school personnel will have to distinguish between chance happenings and those resulting from errors. Too often a person states, "I've just had an accident." He means that he has suffered a misfortune, but he would be more nearly accurate if he terms the occurrence a "mistake." It was his own judgment which was faulty. With reasonable prudence, he should have been able to foresee that the event could happen and probably would happen.

Unavoidable accidents result from circumstances such that neither party can be held guilty of actionable negligence. An accident in this sense is an event, an occurrence. It has the element of chance. Assignable cause is absent; it is just bad fortune. Accidents as such are part and parcel of the vicissitudes of living. Where no negligence can be found, the accident was unavoidable. No liability accrues.

In general, courts are not apt to impose liability against school personnel for injuries to others if (1) the injury sustained is caused by an unavoidable and nonforeseeable accident; (2) the employee's negligence is not the proximate cause of the harm, but an intervening act or event was the real or legal cause; (3) there is contributory negligence on the part of the injured party; and (4) the injured person assumed the risk.

On the other hand, a mistake in operating a motor vehicle is a miscalculation. The result stems from poor or warped judgment. The driver who pulls to the wrong side of the road in the face of oncoming traffic is negligent. This is a mistake, not a true accident.[6] When one "makes a mistake," he can misidentify or err in estimating distances or consequences. He can err in not comprehending or recognizing alternatives. The one who makes a mistake "is, or plays at, cross purposes" with the real world.

Insurance.   The problem of proper protection from automobile-induced injury has assumed great importance. Public education is big business. Most school systems now operate on the basis that the school district is not liable for damages that may occur. However unrealistic this attitude may be, consideration should be given to a means of protection for all concerned. One of the answers to an employee's liability problem in the use of automobiles is holding adequate insurance protection. Insurance and related compensation for pupils and employees are matters that should be thoroughly explored. A personal liability policy is one means of

---

6 *Territo* v. *Carter,* 138 So. (2d) 218 (La., 1962). The doer of the act here blundered, using poor judgment. He was foolish and wholly in the wrong.

safeguarding life earnings and of shouldering one's minimal responsibility toward society.

As long as judges are reluctant to act as lawmakers by overthrowing the long-settled principle of "immunity-from-suit" for torts enjoyed by government, then insurance protects against the disaster of a large verdict. Safeguarding others who must get involved with the educational program is a moral and legal responsibility of the school district. School boards cannot take too much caution to prevent injuries. Injuries still happen. Insurance rightly "spreads the risks involved."

Intentional Injury

Besides liability for carelessness—whether by automobile or other means—there is liability for the class of intentional harm done to others. This means willful and sometimes perverse injury to others, embracing such problems as intended or actual violence to the person of another or to his reputation.

Assault and battery.   These are ordinarily cojoined and thus lead to misunderstandings. A battery is touching another "in a hostile manner." To push gently against another is no battery. To push rudely may justify damages. The attitude of the toucher becomes the determining factor. Even though the touching is severe, it constitutes no battery unless intent to harm is present.

Two kinds of interests are protected in battery. The first is interest of the individual in freedom from bodily harm or any impairment of physical integrity of the person by the infliction thereon of physical pain by another person. The second interest is freedom from bodily touching, although no physical harm is done. This interest is invaded when the touching of the body offends the reasonable sense of personal dignity usually respected in a civilized community.

A battery includes assault, but assault is no battery. The assault alone is any willful or wanton offer—with force or violence—to do a corporal hurt to another, under such circumstances as denote at the time an intention to do it, coupled with a present ability to carry out such intention. An assault is an attempt to commit a battery. In an assault, there is more than playful gesture. The victim does not have to be harmed by attempting to "get away." He does not need to be made unhappy or "put in fear." An assault (a trespass to the person) is committed if, without privilege, a person intends another person to anticipate fairly immediate and unpermitted physical contact. This is so even though the contact is easily avoided and not damageable. In an assault, neither fear nor emotional disturbance is a requisite.

Teachers have been charged with assault and battery of pupils under their control. Where there was no evidence to indicate that the defendant teacher was actuated by any malice (expressed or implied), or of any serious physical injury, or of any punishment in excess of that which the law authorized, trial courts have directed verdicts for the defendant-teachers at the conclusion of state's evidence. The law authorizes teachers who do stand *in loco parentis* to inflict punishment with good faith and a proper motive. Civil suits are brought against teachers for damages on account of injuries to pupils resulting from corporal punishment. If there is no express statute or regulation against the use of physical force, a teacher may use it to discipline pupils. Even where it is prohibited, a teacher may strike a pupil in self-defense. However, if anger or malice can be proved, the principles of common law with regard to reasonable punishment of pupils are of no avail as defense in an assault and battery action.

False imprisonment.   Some cases involve the rights of a parent to visit the public schools. A case in the former Territory of Hawaii concerned a school visit where a parent interfered with the normal functions and duties of school personnel. The parent was asked to leave but refused. Nearby United States Marines were called, and they took the mother away bodily, thus interfering with her freedom to move about. She charged the school administration with false arrest and false imprisonment, insisting she was "unlawfully detained." Her legal base was that one may not detain another, for any length of time, whereby he is deprived of his liberty. Despite an appeal, the plaintiff mother lost her case.

The court held that the school authorities were within their legal limits in ejecting the trouble-maker. This was so even with the exercise of force. An imprisonment is any express or implied threat of force, by which fact the other person is deprived of his liberty, compelled to remain where he does not wish to remain, or go where he does not wish to go.[7] School personnel who choose to detain

---

[7] *In re State in Interest of Cook,* 145 So. (2d) 627 (La., 1962) was a case where a minor was illegally held. He was held in jail because he told officers he was 15 years of age when, in fact, he was 13. The court said he could not complain. The boy was not denied due process under the Fifth Amendment (and made applicable to the states by the Fourteenth) because of the taking of his confession while so held. He readily admitted the matters covered in the confession.

a pupil after school hours face no prospect of liability for imprisonment unless such punishment springs from improper motives.

Protection through Privilege

The law of privileged communication affects the work and responsibility of school personnel. Professional personnel are frequently called upon to make official statements about pupils and other professional employees. These statements are "qualifiedly privileged." The persons making them are generally not held liable in damages—even though the comments they made were false—provided they were not made with malice and bad faith, with the intent to injure.

Such statements, made in the line of duty by a teacher about a pupil, are not actionable because they are "legally protected" utterances. The protection of qualified privilege affords no shield for the teacher if his statements are defamatory and not made in the strict line of professional responsibilities. In other words, the teacher would be liable for those comments. The employee must be careful in exercising the special privileges extended to him so that he might perform his duties more efficiently.

The adjective "defamatory" obviously refers to defamation. This is an attack upon the reputation of another. It includes both slander and libel.[8] Defamation is false telling (a publication by oral or printed means) of something tending to injure the reputation of one now alive and expose him to public hatred, comtempt, or ridicule. Slander, as a part of defamation, is the speaking of base and defamatory words which tend to the prejudice of the reputation, office, trade, business, or means of getting a living of another. It is calculated to bring the injured person into disrepute. "Libel per se" is false and unprivileged printing of unfounded statements exposing a person to hatred, distrust, or obloquy, and which in the natural and proximate consequence will necessarily cause injury. An advertisement which falsely recounted activities of city police on a college campus and elsewhere was called "libelous per se." The libelous matter was connected with the plaintiff in his work as police commissioner. A nonresident who has libel printed beyond the boundaries of the state, and who distributes the libel in the state, is actionable for libel within the state as well as in the state where the slanderous material was printed.

---

[8] Libel must be distinguished from the adjective "liable" related to liability. Libel is written and published slander, which may incur liability.

Summary

Every person is presumed to know the law and is bound at his own peril to heed the public statutes. The law imposes a duty upon individuals to observe impending danger when possible and then to avert injury. Failure to do so constitutes negligence when peril could have been apparent to one causing the injury, had he been maintaining proper vigilance. Teachers must take care in administering "first aid" to pupils and in "giving treatment" to injured pupils. Businesses must abide by standards of care so as not to injure others.

This takes on added significance when it continues to be the pattern in most states that the immunity of a school district (or the board) from liability for personal injuries, sustained by reason of the negligence of officers or employees, applies to injuries occurring on school premises as well as off. In the absence of statute, tort liability rests upon common-law principles which hold the doer of the negligent act to be liable, and which hold government to be exempt from liability for its torts and those of its officers and employees.

One injured through the wrongful act of another, under the law, is entitled to full indemnification for damages. The principle is universal that every individual is personally liable in damages for his acts of carelessness. This basic rule applies equally to school personnel. Their liability is judged by the same set of legal principles that is used for all individuals whose carelessness injures others. An employee of a board may be held responsible in case of injury to a pupil helping move a piano or other piece of equipment. The person requesting the work done is liable if negligence can be proved.

What is the test of personal liability? The act of a teacher becomes negligent by reason of the ability of a prudent teacher, in the exercise of ordinary care, to foresee that harmful results will follow its commission. Every person, school-connected or not, must exercise sense and intelligence to avoid injury to others. Where it appears that investigation and inspection may disclose danger, duty to investigate and inspect arises there. Any culpable cause of injury is actionable. The plaintiff must show (1) that the defendant's intention was unlawful, or (2) that the defendant was at fault. The defendant will not be liable if the injury complained of was unavoidable and the conduct of the defendant free from blame.

When a person's negligent conduct results in injury to another so as to create a cause of action, his liability may have far-reaching consequences. One may be liable in damages for actual physical harm and may also be liable for:

> . . . physical harm from shock or fright; additional bodily injury resulting from acts done by third persons in rendering aid irrespective of whether such acts are done in a proper manner; any disease which is contracted; harm sustained in a subsequent accident which would not have occurred had the health not been impaired by the original negligent act.

All injury that occurs under the jurisdiction of the school should be of the utmost concern to employees, school officers, and boards. First, the types of injuries and where they happen suggest possible changes in procedures, if not in school policy. Second, the question of personal or board liability always makes some of the patrons wonder about the integrity of school leaders, thus lowering the image of education in the eyes of the public. A doubting public hardly needs additional ammunition for its attacks.

The whole subject of torts may be grouped under the premise that each person in society should regulate his own conduct so that it will not interfere unreasonably with the condition or activity of others. This premise also requires that the person shall—if he does not thus regulate his conduct—make reparation for the harm done. Torts include those socially imposed private duties which it seems necessary to assert to promote the common welfare of all. The problem of recognition and enforcement of those duties has more and more become recognized as a problem of social desirability, not as a matter of arranging fixed rules into some logical system.

What is needed now are two things: (1) a general following by all the states of the leadership of New York, and (2) a focus upon the extremely difficult problems of what the limits of such liability ought to be. Is it not agreed that no two nations could solve their problems of responsibility to citizens for injuries in precisely the same way? This, however, is not so where individual state governments are concerned. Here, there are similar circumstances by way of history, national backgrounds, and economic concerns which are common. Only a beginning has been made. All must take the task seriously.

Bibliography

Abraham, Henry J., *Courts and Judges*. New York: Oxford University Press, 1959.

Chamberlain, Leo M. and Leslie W. Kindred, *The Teacher and School Organization*. Englewood Cliffs, N.J.: Prentice-Hall, Inc., 1958.

Cubberley, Ellwood P., *Public Education in the United States*. Boston: Houghton Mifflin Company, 1919.

Edwards, Newton, *The Courts and the Public Schools*, rev. ed. Chicago: The University of Chicago Press, 1955.

————, *The Courts and the Public Schools*. Chicago: The University of Chicago Press, 1935.

Garber, Lee O., ed., *Law and the School Business Manager*. Danville, Ill.: Interstate Printers and Publishers, Inc., 1957.

Gauerke, Warren E., *Legal and Ethical Responsibilities of School Personnel*. Englewood Cliffs, N.J.: Prentice-Hall, Inc., 1959.

Hamilton, Robert, *The Bi-Weekly School Law Letter*, Vol. III, No. 17, October 15, 1953.

Hamilton, Robert R. and Paul R. Mort, *The Law and Public Education*. Chicago: The Foundation Press, Inc., 1941.

Hamilton, Robert R. and E. Edmund Reutter, Jr., *Legal Aspects of School Board Operation*. New York: Bureau of Publications, Teachers College, Columbia University, 1958.

Kramer, Robert, ed., "School Pupils and the Law," *Law and Contemporary Problems*, 20:1–195, Winter, 1955.

Lieberman, Myron, *Education as a Profession*. Englewood Cliffs, N.J.: Prentice-Hall, Inc., 1956.

Mayers, Lewis, *The American Legal System*. New York: Harper and Row, Publishers, 1955.

Price, Miles O. and Harry Bitner, *Effective Legal Research*. Englewood Cliffs, N.J.: Prentice-Hall, Inc., 1953.

Remmlein, Madaline Kinter, *The Law of Local Public School Administration*. New York: McGraw Hill Book Company, 1952.

————, "Tort Liability of School Districts, Boards, and Employees," Chapter VIII, in *Law and the School Business Manager*, ed. Lee O. Garber. Danville, Ill.: Interstate Printers and Publishers, Inc., 1957.

————, "Statutory Problems," *Law and Contemporary Problems*, XX, Winter, 1955.

————, *School Law*, 2nd ed. Danville, Ill.: Interstate Printers and Publishers, Inc., 1962.

Rosenfield, Harry N., *Liability for School Accidents*. New York: Harper & Row, Publishers, 1940.

Seitz, Reynolds C., "Law of Privileged Communications," in *Law and the School Principal*, ed. Seitz. Cincinnati, Ohio: W. H. Anderson Co., 1961.

Voorhees, Harvey C., *The Law and the Public School System of the United States*. Boston: Little, Brown & Co., 1916.

BIBLIOGRAPHY

Weltzin, Joachim Frederic, *The Legal Authority of the American Public School,* rev. ed. Grand Forks, N.D.: The Mid-West Book Concern, 1932.

Wormser, Rene A., *The Law.* New York: Simon and Schuster, Inc., 1949.

Index